FRONTISPIECE. 13½in (34.3cm) Carl Bergner two-face doll showing laughing side of face. (See pages 14, 15 & 18.)

TITLE PAGE. 18in (45.7cm) Kestner 151; bisque socket head, original blonde mohair wig; blue-gray sleep eyes; open/closed mouth; five-piece bent-limb composition body. He is dressed in a white cotton shirt, a brown velvet suit and matching hat.

FRONT COVER. 25in (63.5cm) Kestner 143; bisque socket head, original blonde mohair wig; brown sleep eyes; open mouth with two upper teeth; jointed composition body.

BACK COVER. 13in (33.0cm) Gebruder Heubach 6970. (See pages 28 and 29.)

The Collector's Digest On
German Character Dolls

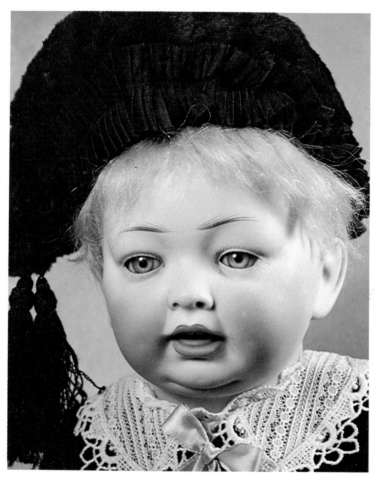

by Robert & Karin MacDowell
photographs by Authors

Published by

HOBBY HOUSE PRESS, INC.
Cumberland, Maryland 21502

Dedication

To Gladys MacDowell and to our sons Karl, Mark and Gordon.

Acknowledgements

Considering the scarcity of fine, authentic examples of antique dolls of all types and, especially the lack of concise photographic material, a book of this type would be severely limited were it not for the extreme generosity and goodwill shown by our many friends, clients and colleagues.

Rather than list all of our contributors, we have given credit with the illustrations. Since we have taken all of the photographs - mostly in our studio - many of the dolls have been brought here by their owners for the sole purpose of providing material for this book. We are especially grateful for the extra effort this has involved.

At the time the photographs were taken the ownership of the dolls was as stated with the photographs. Where ownership is not stated, dolls were from the MacDowell Doll Museum Collection. Since dolls are constantly changing hands, there will be many changes by the time this book is printed.

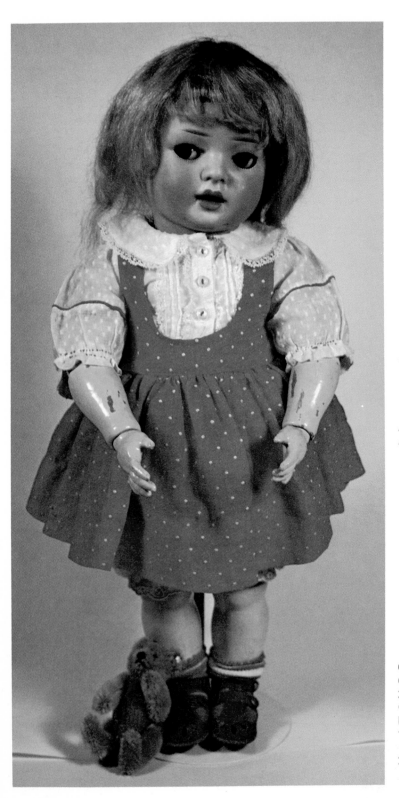

Color Illustration
1. 16in (40.6cm)
Schönau &
Hoffmeister
Hanna. *Gladys
MacDowell Col-
lection.* (See page
128.)

OPPOSITE PAGE
Color Illustration
2. 12in (30.5cm)
Gebrüder Heu-
bach 78D4
"Laughing Boy."
(See pages 26 &
27.)

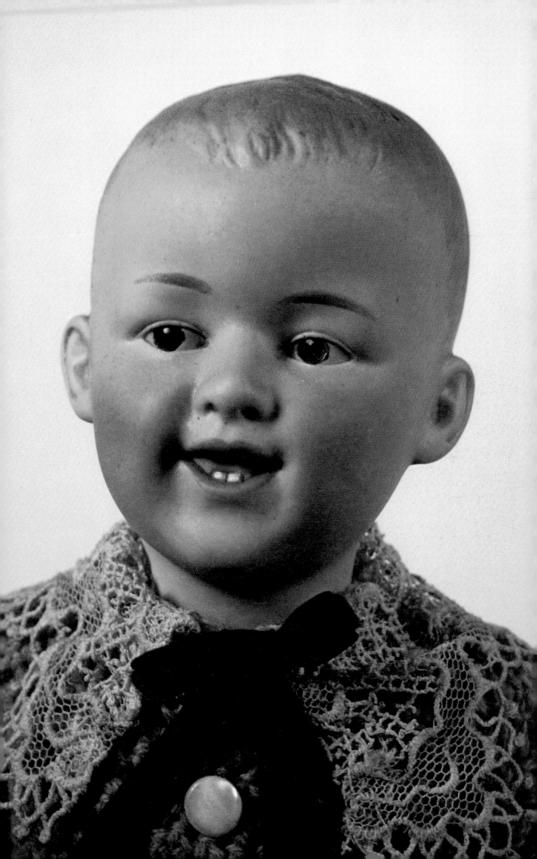

Table Of Contents

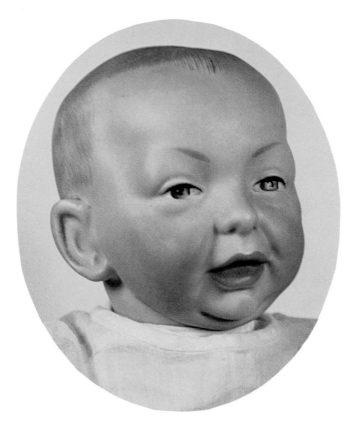

Color Illustration 3. 14in (35.6cm) Kämmer & Reinhardt 100 "Kaiser Baby." (See pages 48 & 49.)

Introduction

During the course of directing an active doll museum, there is an unusual degree of exposure to a fascinating variety of material. One primary goal of any museum should be the collection and distribution of valid information. This book contains data available to us up to October 1980 on the title subject.

For consistency, we define German Character Dolls as those made in Germany, regardless of the origin of their design. "Character" implies a departure from the usual sweet/pretty face, with a strong expression or resemblance to a living (or legendary) person. Many of these dolls were originally modeled from living subjects.

Placing a doll in the correct category is not always easy, as there are those which do not possess such strong character features. For example, we have included several specimens which might be considered by others as "ethnic," for example the Heubach/Köppelsdorf black dolls. These have "character" expressions.

All of the dolls included here were considered original, except for costuming. We have not intentionally shown any cases where bodies and heads do not belong together. None of the bodies are repainted, nor are any marks altered in any way.

Should you have a head/body combination which does not agree with an example shown, we must emphasize that quite a lot of variation was common in original assembly. For example, the Kämmer & Reinhardt 126 is shown on a five-piece bent-limb composition body and also on a composition toddler body. Such variations add considerably to the interest and pleasure derived from working with the older dolls.

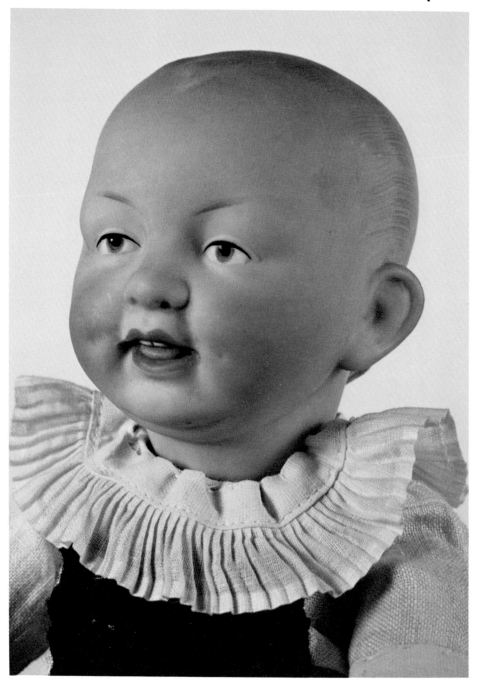

Color Illustration 4. 11in (27.9cm) Alt, Beck & Gottschalck 1322/1.

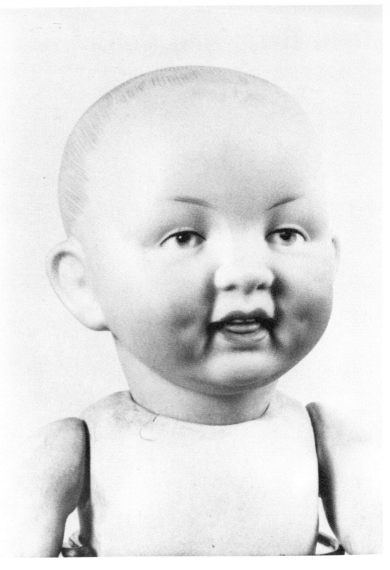

Illustration 1. 11in (27.9cm) Alt, Beck & Gottschalck 1322/1.
Head incised: **A. B. & G.**
        1322/1
        Deponiert
Solid dome bisque socket head, painted molded hair; painted blue intaglio eyes, very finely painted feathered eyebrows; open/closed mouth with molded tongue and two upper teeth; very chubby composition toddler body with straight wrists.

Illustration 2. 11in (27.9cm) Alt, Beck & Gottschalck 1322/1 mark.

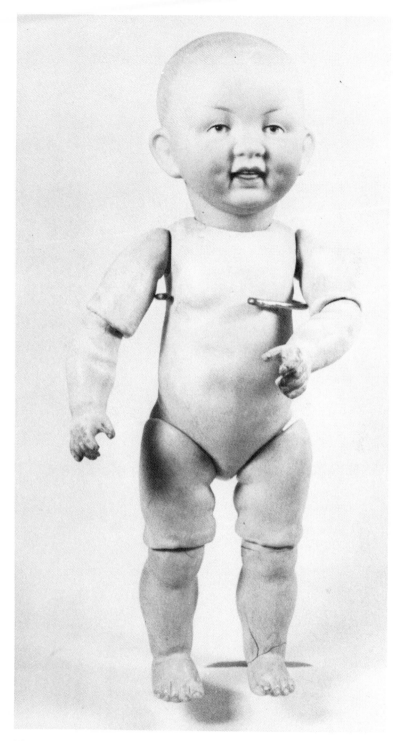

Illustration 3. 11in (27.9cm) Alt, Beck & Gottschalck 1322/1 shown undressed. Note fine details of chubby toddler body.

Color Illustration 5. 10½in (26.7cm) Franz Schmidt & Co. 1295 twins. (See pages 125 through 127.)

Color Illustration 6. 17in (43.2cm) Georgene Averill baby.

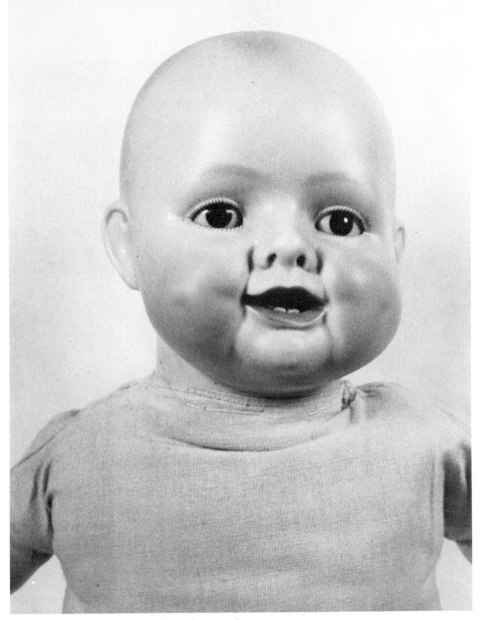

Illustration 4. 17in (43.2cm) (12in [30.5cm] head circumference) Georgene Averill baby.
Head incised: **Copr. by**
                    Georgene Averill
                    1005/3652
                    Germany
Solid dome bisque head with flange neck, painted hair; blue sleep eyes; open mouth with two lower teeth, wobbly tongue; cloth body with crier box; composition arms and legs. Most of these dolls are found with arms and legs in rather poor condition. Very often they are crazed or chipped.

Illustration 5. 17in (43.2cm) Georgene Averill baby mark.

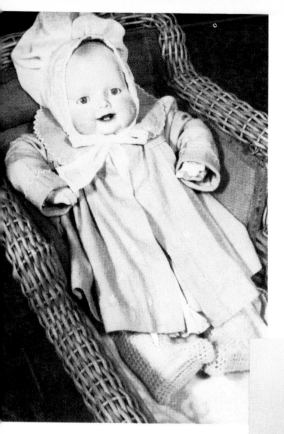

Illustration 6. 17in (43.2cm) Georgene Averill baby wearing a white cotton dress and bonnet and a blue wool coat with white embroidered flowers.

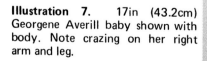

Illustration 7. 17in (43.2cm) Georgene Averill baby shown with body. Note crazing on her right arm and leg.

Color Illustration 7. 11in (27.9cm) Kämmer & Reinhardt 100 "Kaiser Baby;" solid dome bisque socket head, painted hair; blue intaglio eyes; open/closed mouth; five-piece bent-limb composition body. He is dressed in a beautiful white gown with matching bonnet.

Color Illustration 8. 12in (30.5cm) Kämmer & Reinhardt 121; bisque socket head, original blonde mohair wig; blue sleep eyes, feathered eyebrows; open mouth with two upper teeth, wobbly tongue; composition toddler body. A nice small size that is rather difficult to find. She wears a cream colored dress with matching lace, cotton sox and imitation leather shoes.

Baby Phyllis

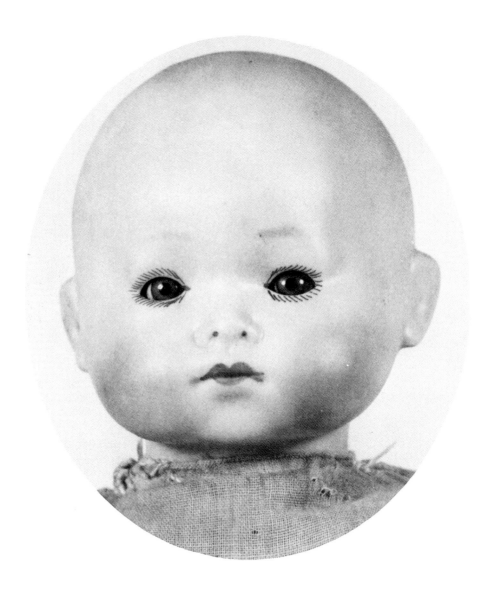

Illustration 8. 10in (25.4cm) *Baby Phyllis*, made by Armand Marseille.
Head incised:

Baby Phyllis
Made in Germany

Solid dome head with flange neck, painted hair; blue sleep eyes, closed mouth;
cloth body with voice box; composition hands. *Lillian J. Mote Collection.*

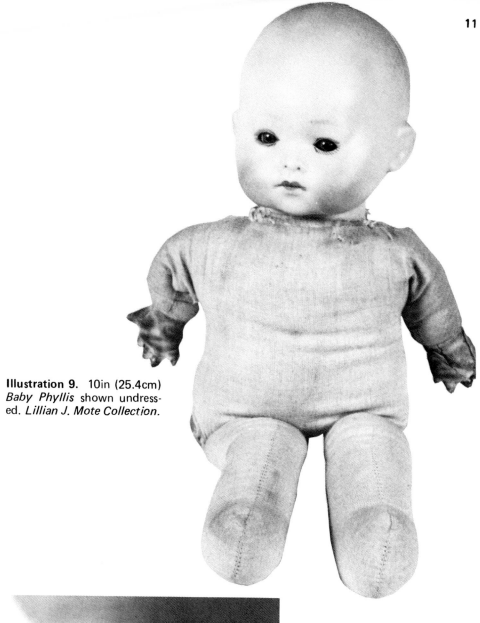

Illustration 9. 10in (25.4cm) *Baby Phyllis* shown undressed. *Lillian J. Mote Collection.*

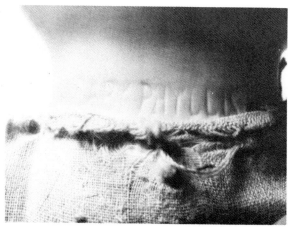

Illustration 10. 10in (25.4cm) *Baby Phyllis* mark. *Lillian J. Mote Collection.*

Color Illustration 9. 10in (25.4cm) Armand Marseille *Dream Baby* 341; marked: "A M//Germany//341. 1316;" solid dome bisque head with flange neck; blue sleep eyes; closed mouth; cloth body with composition hands. She is dressed in a white lawn short gown, a pink wool crocheted jacket, bonnet and sox.

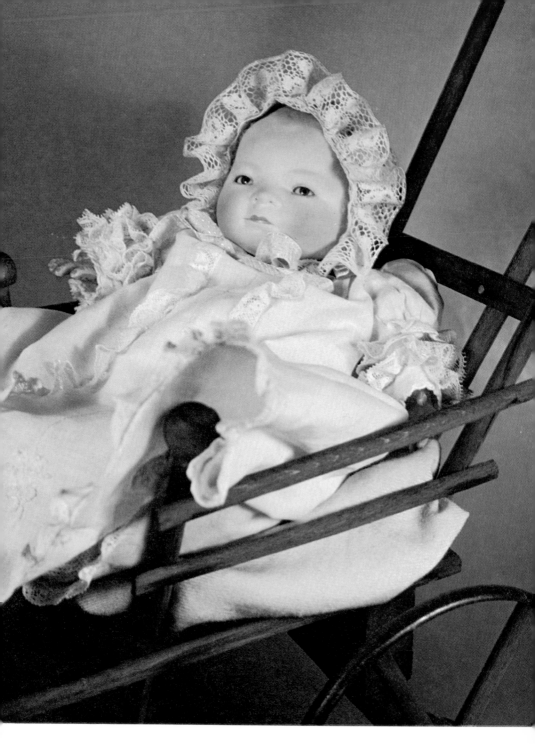

Color Illustration 10. 9in (22.9cm) *Bye-Lo Baby;* head marked: "Copr. by//
Grace S. Putnam//Germany;" solid dome bisque head with flange neck, painted
molded hair; blue sleep eyes; single stroke eyebrows; closed mouth; cloth body
with celluloid hands; dressed in white lawn gown and bonnet with lots of lace and
pink ribbon.

Illustration 11. 13½in (34.3cm) Carl Bergner two-face doll.
Shoulder plate marked:

Two-face bisque socket head, one smiling, one crying; original blonde mohair wig. The crying side has blue sleep eyes, feathered eyebrows; open/closed mouth. Note tiny molded tears under eyelids. Hood and shoulder plate are composition; cloth over cardboard body with composition arms and legs.

Illustration 12. 13½in (34.3cm) Carl Bergner two-face doll mark on back of composition shoulder plate.

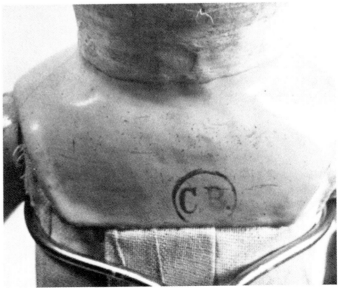

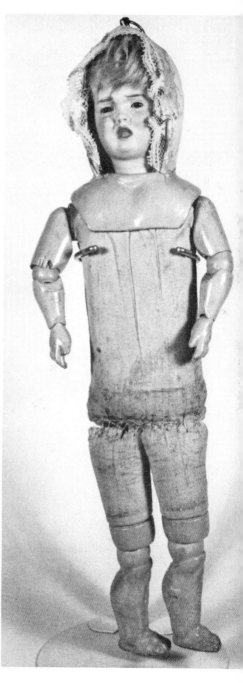

Illustration 13. 13½in (34.3cm) Carl Bergner two-face doll showing smiling face, original blonde mohair wig; blue sleep eyes, feathered eyebrows; open/closed mouth. Note unusual modeling which accentuates cheek contours. The bisque on this doll is very smooth and fine.

Illustration 14. 13½in (34.3cm) Carl Bergner two-face doll shown undressed.

Color Illustration 12. 9in (22.9cm) Gebrüder Heubach 8192; bisque socket head; mohair wig; blue sleep eyes, single stroke eyebrows; open mouth; composition body with straight arms and legs; painted sox and shoes. She is dressed in blue silk with added ecru crocheting.

Color Illustration 11. 13in (33.0cm) Gebrüder Heubach "Coquette." (See pages 34 & 35.)

Color Illustration 13. 13½in (34.3cm) Kämmer & Reinhardt 126; human hair wig; wearing her original dress of blue organdy and imitation white leather shoes. (See pages 66 & 67.)

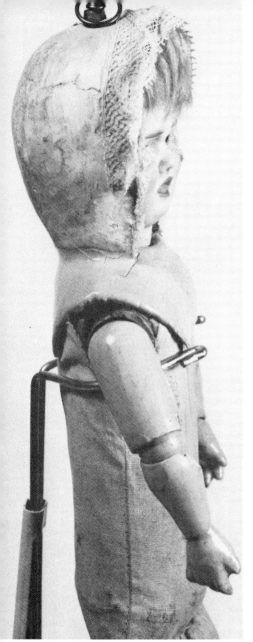

Illustration 15. 13½in (34.3cm) Carl Bergner two-face doll shown with hood and shoulder plate and construction of upper body.

Illustration 16. 13½in (34.3cm) Carl Bergner two-face doll originally dressed in a white baby gown with blue ribbons and a lace covered hood.

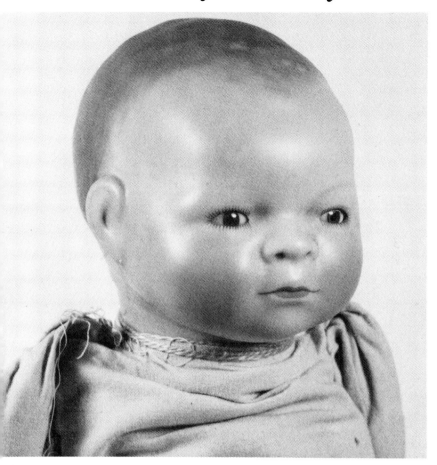

Illustration 17. 12½in (31.8cm) head circumference *Bye-Lo Baby*.
Head incised:

Copr. by
Grace S. Putnam
Germany

Bisque head with flange neck, painted hair; blue sleep eyes, single stroke eyebrows; closed mouth; cloth body with celluloid hands (turtle mark).

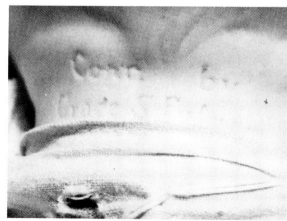

Illustration 18. 12½in (31.8cm) head circumference *Bye-Lo Baby* mark on head. There are numbers and "Made in Germany" under the "Grace S. Putnam" which are covered up by the cloth body.

Color Illustration 14. 21½in (54.6cm) Simon & Halbig 151. *Gladys MacDowell Collection.* (See pages 129 through 131.)

Color Illustration 15. 14in (35.6cm) Simon & Halbig 1468 "Flapper." *Gladys MacDowell Collection.* (See page 136.)

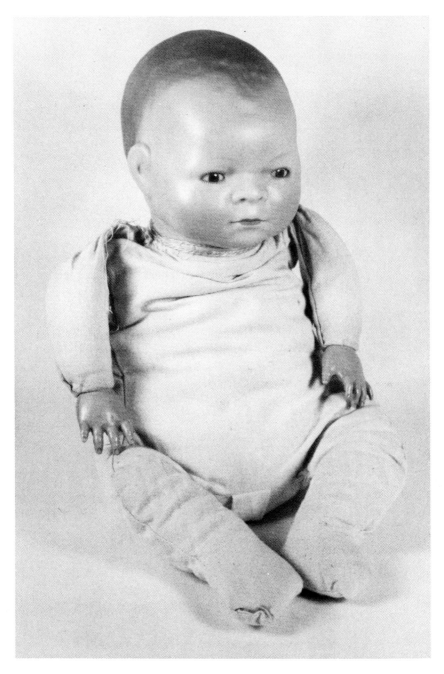

Illustration 19. 12½in (31.8cm) head circumference *Bye-Lo Baby* with cloth body and celluloid hands.

Cuno & Otto Dressel 1469 "Flapper"

Illustration 20. 14in (35.6cm) Cuno & Otto Dressel 1469, commonly called "Flapper." Head incised:
1469.
C. & O. Dressel.
Germany.
2.
Bisque socket head, original mohair wig; brown sleep eyes with original lashes, single stroke eyebrows; closed mouth; lady-type body with molded bust, very slender waist and long thin arms and legs (see A M "Flapper," pages 106, 107).

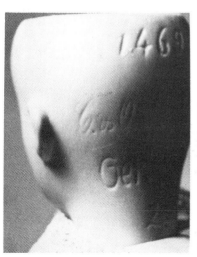

Illustration 21. 14in (35.6cm) Cuno & Otto Dressel 1469 "Flapper" mark.

Illustration 22.
14in (35.6cm)
Cuno & Otto
Dressel 1469
"Flapper,"
shown in her
original cream-
colored satin and
net dress, silk
stockings and
leather shoes. It
is rather unusual
to find the shoes
still on the doll;
the originals are
generally missing.

Gebrüder Heubach "Googly"

Illustration 23. 7½in (19.1cm) Gebrüder Heubach, commonly called "Googly."
Head incised:

            5/o D

90	HEU BACH	56

Germany

Bisque socket head, painted molded hair; painted blue intaglio eyes, single stroke eyebrows; watermelon mouth; five-piece bent-limb composition body.

Illustration 24. 7½in (19.1cm) Gebrüder Heubach "Googly" in a pale pink dress with white cotton trim.

Gebrüder Heubach 78D4
"Laughing Boy"

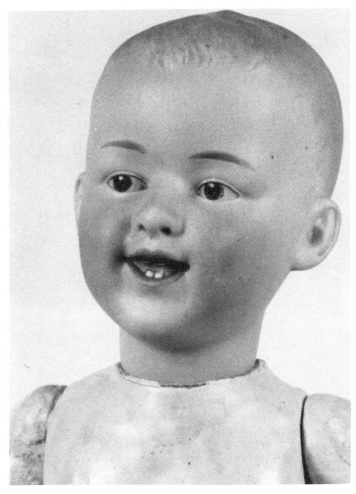

Illustration 25. 12in (30.5cm) Gebrüder Heubach 78D4, commonly called "Laughing Boy." Head incised:

4
Germany
78D4

Bisque socket head, painted molded hair; painted blue intaglio eyes, single stroke eyebrows; open/closed mouth with two lower molded teeth; five-piece bent-limb composition body.

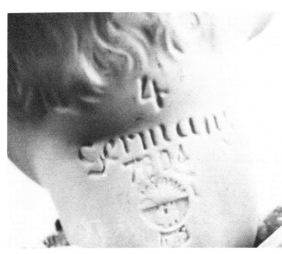

Illustration 26. 12in (30.5cm) Gebrüder Heubach 78D4 "Laughing Boy" mark.

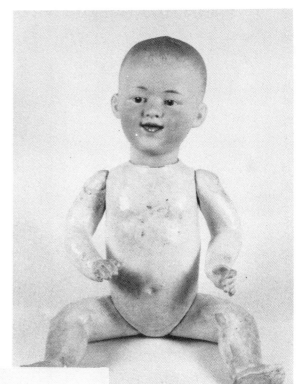

Illustration 27. 12in (30.5cm) Gebrüder Heubach 78D4 "Laughing Boy" shown with bent-limb body.

Illustration 28. 12in (30.5cm) Gebrüder Heubach 78D4 "Laughing Boy" dressed in crocheted light brown wool jacket and pants.

Gebrüder Heubach 6970

OPPOSITE PAGE: Illustration 31.
13in (33.0cm) Gebrüder Heubach 6970.
Head incised: **6970**
4
Germany

Bisque socket head, blonde mohair wig; blue sleep eyes, feathered eyebrows; closed mouth; fully-jointed composition body.

Illustration 29. 13in (33.0cm) Gebrüder Heubach 6970 shown in a light blue organdy dress with white lace and matching hat.

Illustration 30. 13in (33.0cm) Gebrüder Heubach 6970 mark.

Gebrüder Heubach   7246

Illustration 32. 21in (53.3cm)
Gebrüder Heubach 7246.
Head incised: **7246**
        8
     Germany

Bisque socket head (the bisque is
pre-colored pink), human hair wig;
brown sleep eyes, feathered eyebrows; deeply modeled nostrils;
closed pouty mouth; jointed composition and wood body.

Illustration 33. 21in (53.3cm)
Gebrüder   Heubach   **7246**
mark.

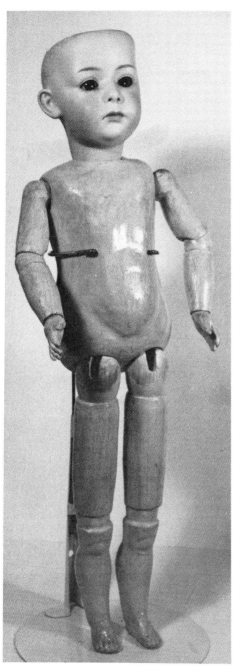

Illustration 34. 21in (53.3cm)
Gebrüder Heubach 7246 on wood
and composition jointed body.

Illustration 35. 21in (53.3cm)
Gebrüder Heubach 7246 dressed in
white lawn dress.

Gebrüder Heubach 8192

Illustration 36. 6½in (16.5cm) Gebrüder Heubach 8192 shown in original clothes of ecru lace and pink satin ribbons.

Illustration 37. 6½in (16.5cm) Gebrüder Heuback 8192 mark.

Illustration 38. 6½in (16.5cm) Gebrüder Heubach 8192.
Head incised:
8192
Gebr. Heubach
Germany
$$\frac{14}{9}$$
Bisque socket head, original mohair wig; blue sleep eyes, single stroke eyebrows; closed mouth; five-piece straight-limb composition body; painted sox and shoes.

Illustration 39. 13in (33.0cm) Gebrüder Heubach, commonly called "Coquette."
Head incised:

7. 3
63

Germany

Bisque socket head, painted molded hair with turquoise ribbon; painted blue intaglio eyes, single stroke eyebrows; open/closed mouth with tiny molded teeth; fully-jointed wood and composition body with stick legs.

Illustration 40. 13in (33.0cm) Gebrüder Heubach "Coquette" mark.

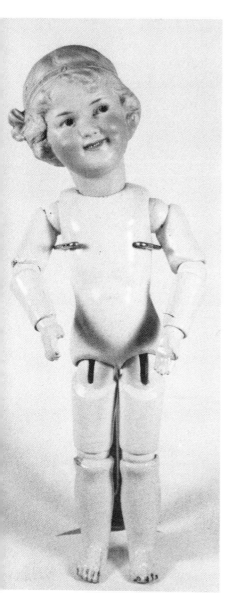

Illustration 42. 13in (33.0cm) Gebrüder Heubach "Coquette" shown in a white cotton dress with insertion lace.

Illustration 41. 13in (33.0cm) Gebrüder Heubach "Coquette" shown undressed.

Gebrüder Heubach "Crooked Smile"

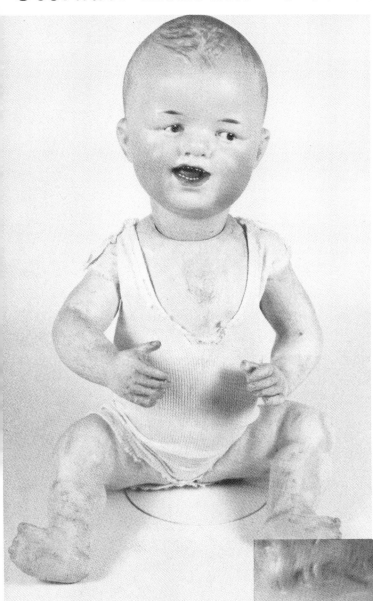

OPPOSITE PAGE:
Illustration 45.
12in (30.5cm) Gebrüder Heubach, commonly called "Crooked Smile." Head incised:

4

8. 9

Germany
Solid dome bisque socket head, painted molded hair; painted blue intaglio eyes, single stroke eyebrows; open/closed mouth with upper and lower tiny molded teeth; five-piece bent-limb composition body. *Gladys MacDowell Collection.*

Illustration 43. 12in (30.5cm) Gebrüder Heubach "Crooked Smile" with bent-limb composition body, dressed in cotton undies.

Illustration 44. 12in (30.5cm) Gebrüder Heubach "Crooked Smile" mark. *Gladys MacDowell Collection.*

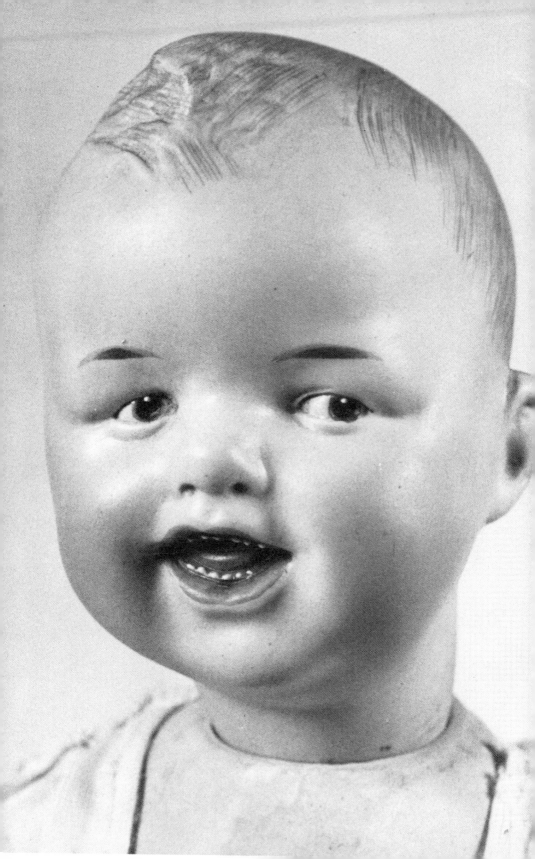

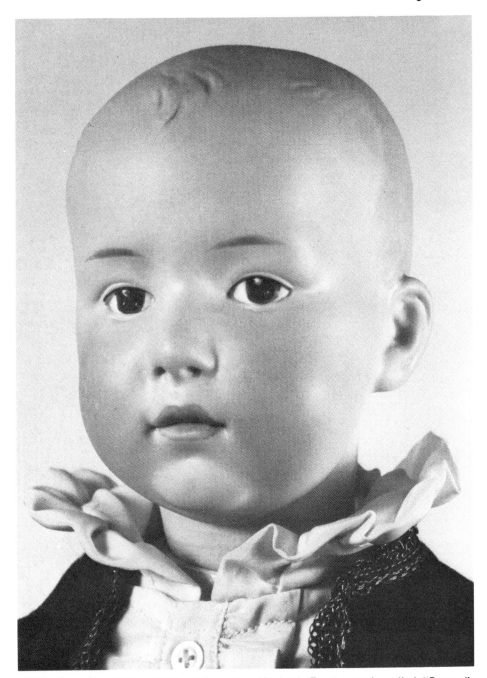

Illustration 46. 18½in (47.0cm) Gebrüder Heubach 7, commonly called "Pouty."
Head incised: **Germany**
                                                7

62

Solid dome bisque head (bisque is pre-tinted pink), painted molded hair; blue intaglio eyes, single stroke eyebrows; open/closed mouth, illusion of tongue; jointed composition and wood body.

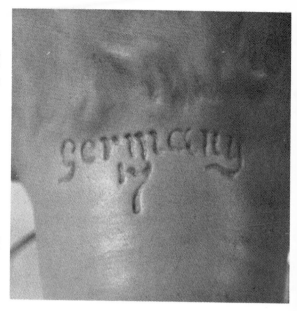

Illustration 47. 18½in (47.0cm) Gebrüder Heubach 7 "Pouty" mark. (The number "62" does not appear in this photo of the mark.)

Illustration 48. 18½in (47.0cm) Gebrüder Heubach 7 "Pouty." Detail of intaglio eyes.

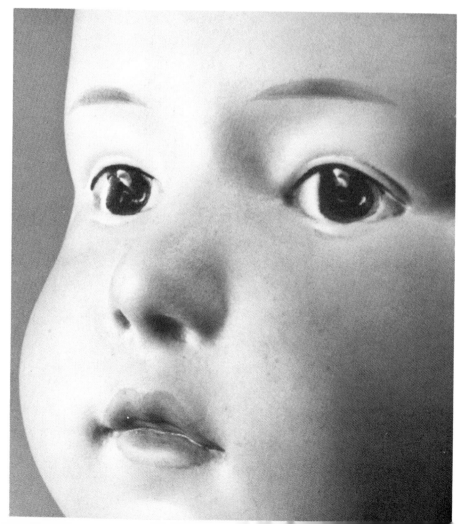

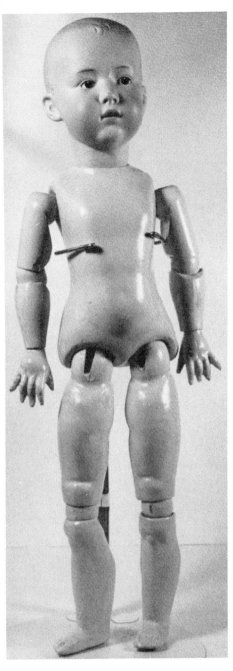

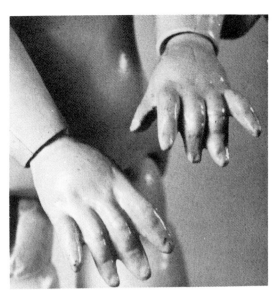

Illustration 50. 18½in (47.0cm) Gebrüder Heubach 7 "Pouty." Note fine details of hands.

Illustration 49. 18½in (47.0cm) Gebrüder Heubach 7 "Pouty" shown undressed on wood and composition body.

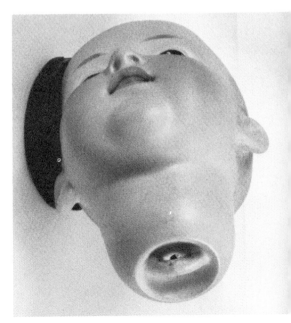

Illustration 51. 18½in (47.0cm) Gebrüder Heubach 7 "Pouty." Note bisque loop inside neck socket for stringing, a very unusual feature.

Illustration 52.
18½in (47.0cm)
Gebrüder Heu-
bach 7 "Pouty"
dressed in white
cotton shirt, red
velvet suit, cotton
sox and black
leather shoes.

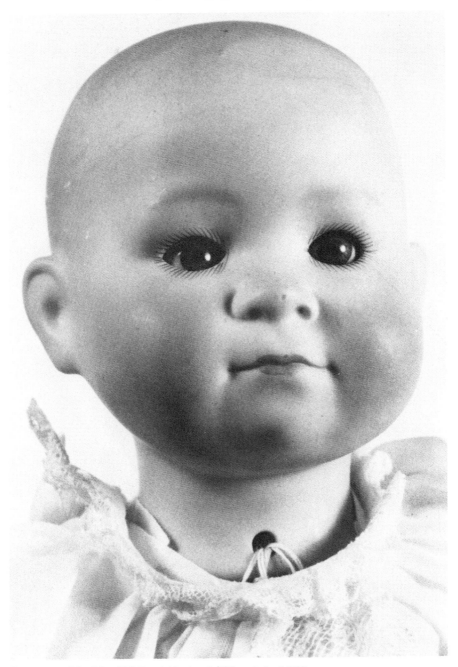

Illustration 53. 12in (30.5cm) Heubach/Köppelsdorf 339.
Head incised: **Heubach Köppelsdorf**
                                       339 . 5/0
                                       Germany
Solid dome bisque head with flange neck, painted hair; blue sleep eyes, single stroke
eyebrows; closed mouth; cloth body with straight legs, celluloid hands; voice box.
Jean Steele Collection.

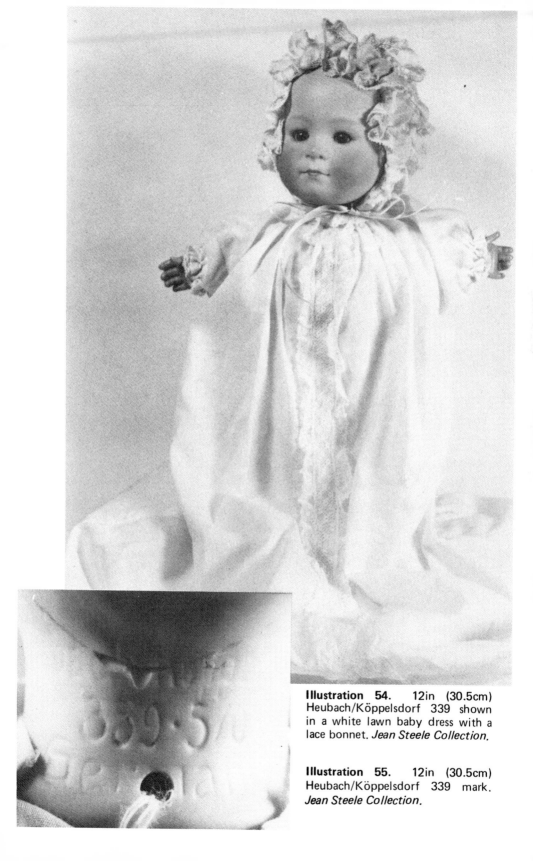

Illustration 54. 12in (30.5cm) Heubach/Köppelsdorf 339 shown in a white lawn baby dress with a lace bonnet. *Jean Steele Collection.*

Illustration 55. 12in (30.5cm) Heubach/Köppelsdorf 339 mark. *Jean Steele Collection.*

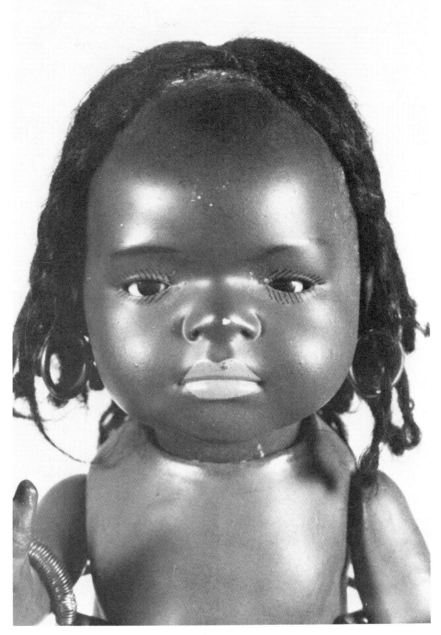

Illustration 56. 14in (35.6cm) Heubach/Köppelsdorf 399.
Head incised: **Heubach. Köppelsdorf**
                                    399 6/o
                                   Germany
Solid dome black bisque socket head, painted black hair, mohair wig attached to head; brown sleep eyes, single stroke eyebrows; closed mouth; pierced ears; black five-piece composition body with straight legs. Paint on head is not fired on; therefore, flaking has occurred (see mark where paint is partially gone). *Gladys MacDowell Collection.*

Illustration 57. 14in (35.6cm) Heubach/Köppelsdorf 399 shown undressed. *Gladys MacDowell Collection.*

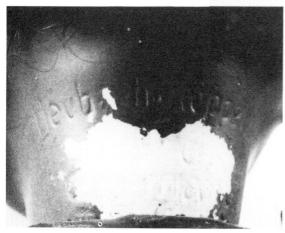

Illustration 58. 14in (35.6cm) Heubach/Köppelsdorf 399 mark on head where paint is partially gone. *Gladys MacDowell Collection.*

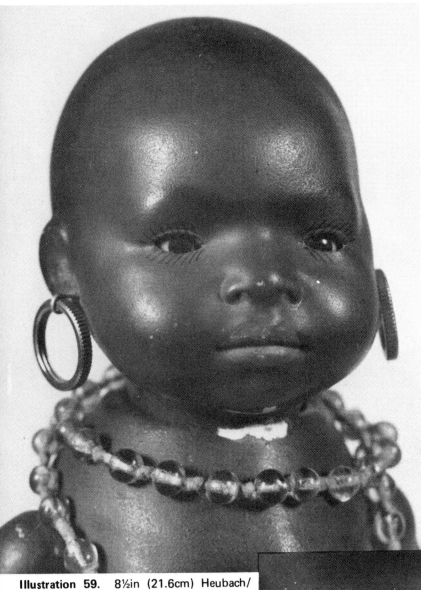

Illustration 59. 8½in (21.6cm) Heubach/ Köppelsdorf 399.
Head incised:
Heubach·Köppelsdorf
399 14/0 D·R·G·M·
Germany
Solid dome black bisque socket head, painted black hair; brown sleep eyes, single stroke eyebrows; closed mouth; pierced ears; black five-piece composition body with bent legs. Paint on this head is not fired on. *Gladys MacDowell Collection.*

Illustration 60. 8½in (21.6cm) Heubach/ Köppelsdorf 399 mark. *Gladys MacDowell Collection.*

Illustration 61. 8½in (21.6cm) Heubach/Köppelsdorf 399 shown undressed. *Gladys MacDowell Collection.*

Illustration 62. 8½in (21.6cm) Heubach/Köppelsdorf 399 all original with brass earrings, glass bead necklace and grass skirt. *Gladys MacDowell Collection.*

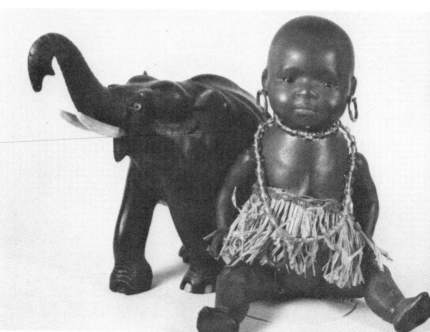

Kämmer & Reinhardt 100
"Kaiser Baby"

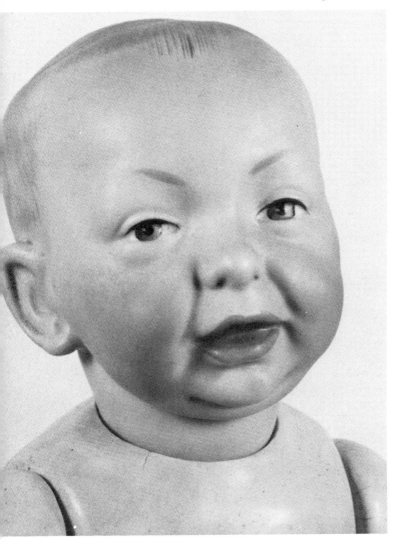

Illustration 63.
14in (35.6cm) (10½in [26.7cm] head circumference) Kämmer & Reinhardt 100, commonly called "Kaiser Baby." Head incised:

36

K R

100

Solid dome bisque socket head, painted molded hair, painted blue intaglio eyes, single stroke eyebrows; open/closed mouth; five-piece bent-limb composition body.

Illustration 64. 14in (35.6cm) Kämmer & Reinhardt 100 "Kaiser Baby" mark.

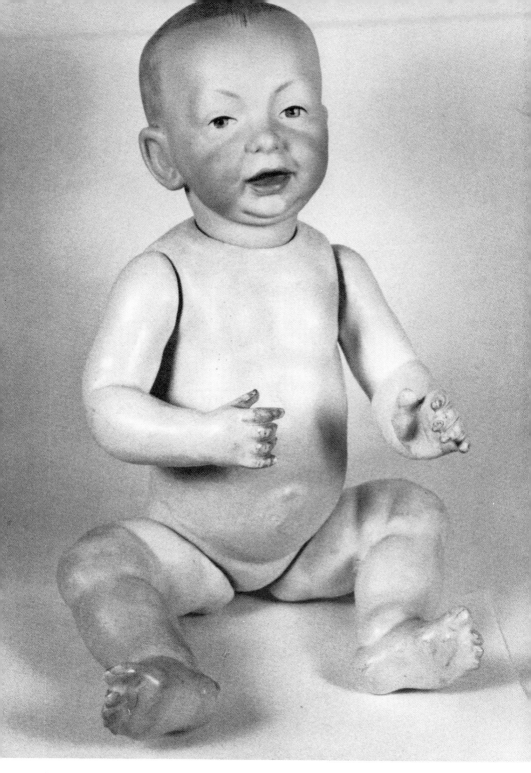

Illustration 65. 14in (35.6cm) Kämmer & Reinhardt 100 "Kaiser Baby" shown with body. Note beautifully modeled body including upturned big toes on feet.

Illustration 66. 12½in (31.8cm) Kämmer & Reinhardt 101 *Marie.*
Head incised:

K ✡ & R
101
34

Bisque socket head, original medium blonde mohair wig with braids; painted blue eyes, single stroke eyebrows; closed mouth; fully-jointed composition body.

Illustration 67. 12½in (31.8cm) Kämmer & Reinhardt 101 *Marie* mark.

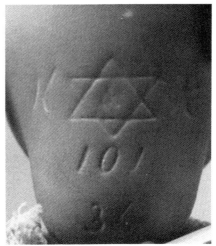

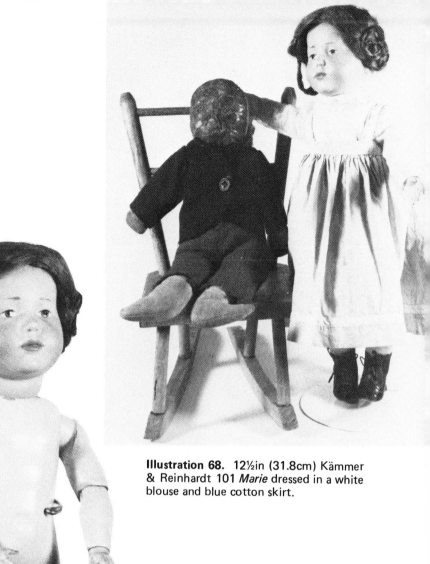

Illustration 68. 12½in (31.8cm) Kämmer & Reinhardt 101 *Marie* dressed in a white blouse and blue cotton skirt.

Illustration 69. 12½in (31.8cm) Kämmer & Reinhardt 101 *Marie* shown with body.

Kämmer & Reinhardt 114 Gretchen

Illustration 70. 13½in (34.3cm) Kämmer & Reinhardt 114 *Gretchen* shown in a white sleeveless cotton dress with pink net overdress, matching sox and leather shoes.

OPPOSITE PAGE: Illustration 71. 13½in (34.3cm) Kämmer & Reinhardt 114 *Gretchen.* Head incised:

K R

114

Bisque socket head, human hair wig; painted blue eyes, single stroke eyebrows; closed mouth; fully-jointed composition body.

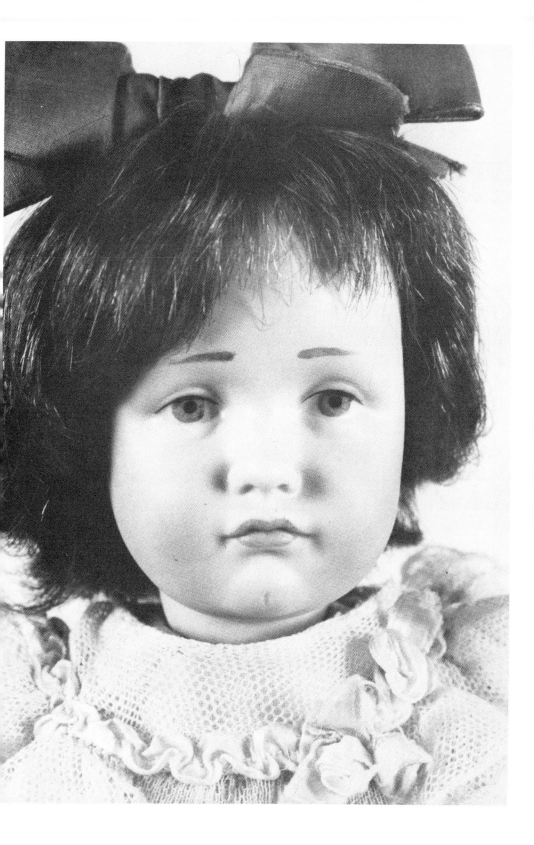

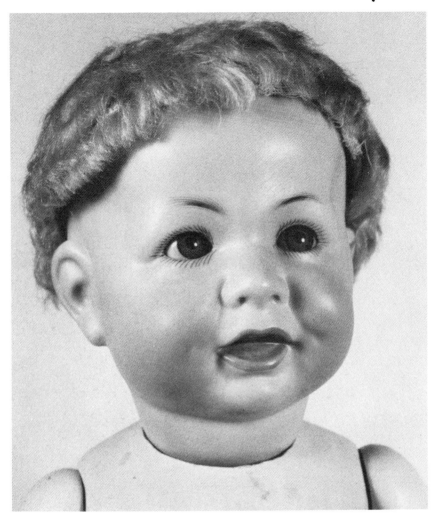

Illustration 72. 16½in (41.9cm)
Kämmer & Reinhardt 116/A.
Head incised:

K   ✡   R

**Simon & Halbig
116/A
42**

Bisque socket head, original blonde
mohair wig; blue sleep eyes,
feathered eyebrows; open/closed
mouth with two upper tiny molded
teeth; composition toddler body
with straight wrists.

Illustration 73. 16½in (41.9cm) Kämmer & Reinhardt
116/A mark. (The number "42" does not appear in
this photo of the mark.)

Illustration 74. 16½in (41.9cm) Kämmer & Reinhardt 116/A dressed in brown linen suit.

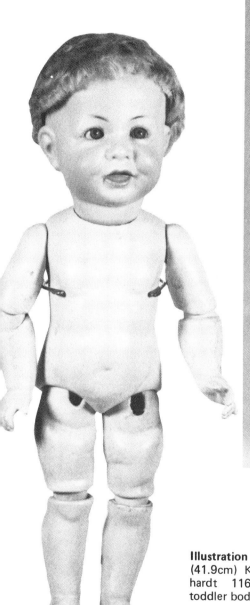

Illustration 75. 16½in (41.9cm) Kämmer & Reinhardt 116/A shown with toddler body.

Kämmer & Reinhardt 117 Mein Liebling

Illustration 76. 23in (58.4cm) Kämmer & Reinhardt 117 *Mein Liebling.*
Head incised:

K ✡& R

Simon & Halbig
117
62

Bisque socket head, human hair wig; brown sleep eyes, feathered eyebrows; closed mouth; jointed composition body.

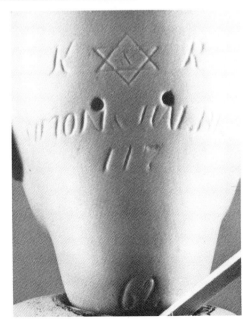

Illustration 77. 23in (58.4cm) Kämmer & Reinhardt 117 *Mein Liebling* mark.

Illustration 78. 23in (58.4cm) Kämmer & Reinhardt 117 *Mein Liebling* wearing a blue organdy dress with white lace and peach colored ribbons.

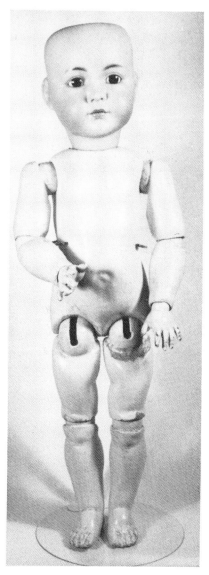

Illustration 79. 23in (58.4cm) Kämmer & Reinhardt 117 *Mein Liebling* shown undressed.

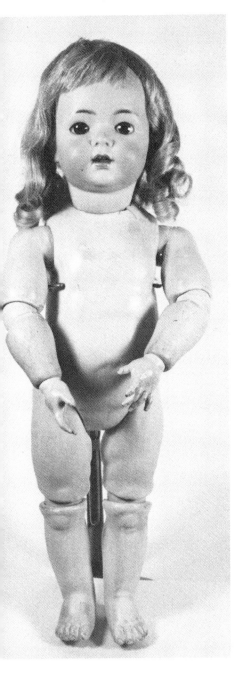

Illustration 80.
18in (45.7cm) Kämmer & Reinhardt 121 shown on toddler body.

Illustration 81.
18in (45.7cm) Kämmer & Reinhardt 121 in yellow and white cotton and satin striped dress and bonnet.

Illustration 82. 18in (45.7cm) Kämmer & Reinhardt 121.
Head incised:

K   ✡   R

Simon & Halbig
121
36

Bisque socket head, human hair wig; brown sleep eyes, feathered eyebrows, painted lower eyelashes only; open mouth with two upper teeth, wobbly tongue; fully-jointed composition toddler body.

Illustraiton 83. 18in (45.7cm) Kämmer & Reinhardt 121 mark. (The number "36" does not appear in this photo of the mark.)

Illustration 84. 18in (45.7cm) Kämmer & Reinhardt 122.
Head incised:

K ✡ R

Simon & Halbig
122
42

Bisque socket head, original mohair wig; blue flirty eyes, feathered eyebrows; open mouth with two rows of teeth, wobbly tongue; composition toddler body. *Gladys MacDowell Collection.*

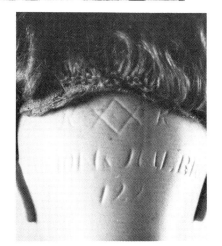

Illustration 85. 18in (45.7cm) Kämmer & Reinhardt 122 mark. (The number "42" does not appear in this photo of the mark.) *Gladys MacDowell Collection.*

Illustration 86.
18in (45.7cm)
Kämmer & Rein-
hardt 122 shown
in a frail silk
dress and cotton
hat. *Gladys
MacDowell Col-
lection.*

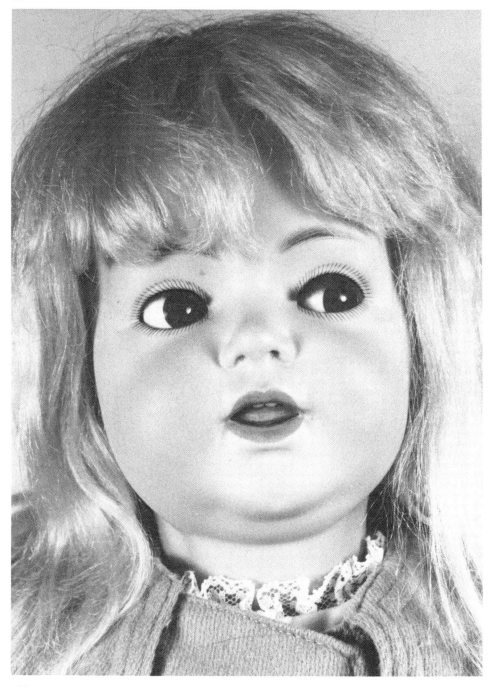

Illustration 87. 24in (61.0cm) Kämmer & Reinhardt 122. Bisque socket head, blonde mohair wig; brown flirty eyes with lashes, feathered eyebrows; open mouth, two upper teeth, wobbly tongue; composition toddler body. *Gladys MacDowell Collection.*

Head incised:

K   R

Simon & Halbig
122

Illustration 88.
24in (61.0cm)
Kämmer & Reinhardt 122 mark.
Gladys MacDowell Collection.

Illustration 89. 24in (61.0cm) Kämmer & Reinhardt 122 dressed in a brown wool coat. *Gladys MacDowell Collection.*

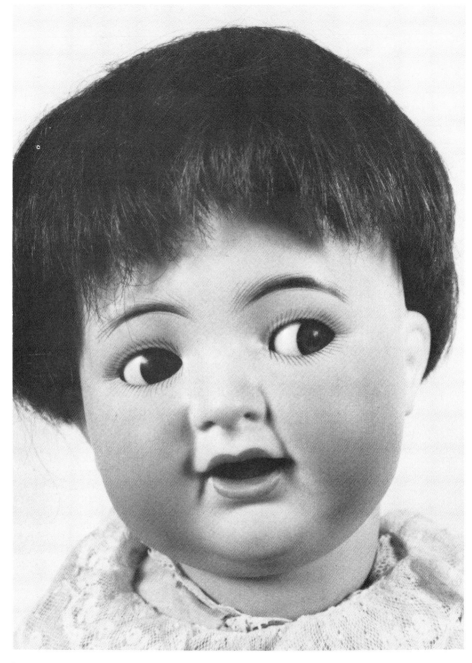

Illustration 90. 21in (53.3cm) Kämmer & Reinhardt 126.
Bisque socket head, human hair wig; blue flirty eyes,
feathered eyebrows; open mouth, two upper teeth, wobbly
tongue; five-piece bent-limb composition body.

Head incised:

K ✡ R

Simon & Halbig
126
Germany
50

Illustration 91. 21in (53.3cm) Kämmer & Reinhardt 126 mark.

Illustration 92. 21in (53.3cm) Kämmer & Reinhardt 126 shown wearing her original pale blue lawn dress and bonnet trimmed with white lace, original sox and replaced shoes.

Illustration 93. A look inside 21in (53.3cm) Kämmer & Reinhardt 126 to show the flirty eye mechanism which appears very complicated.

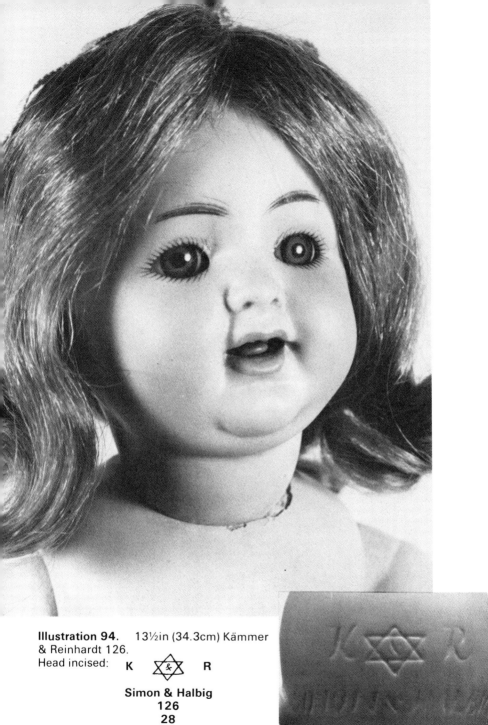

Illustration 94. 13½in (34.3cm) Kämmer & Reinhardt 126.

Head incised: K ✡&✡ R

Simon & Halbig
126
28

Bisque socket head, human hair wig; blue sleep eyes, feathered eyebrows; open mouth, two upper teeth, wobbly tongue; fully-jointed toddler composition body.

Illustration 95. 13½in (34.3cm) Kämmer & Reinhardt 126 mark. (The number "28" does not appear in this photo of the mark.)

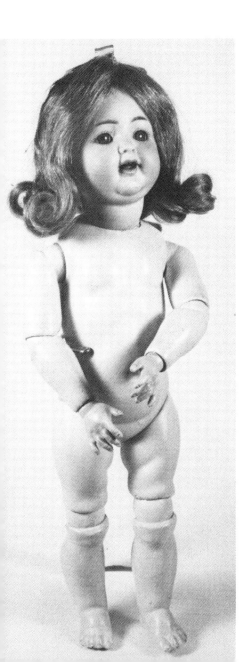

Illustration 96. 13½in (34.3cm) Kämmer & Reinhardt 126 shown in original blue organdy dress with lace and applied flowers.

Illustration 97. 13½in (34.3cm) Kämmer & Reinhardt 126 shown with toddler body.

OPPOSITE PAGE:
Illustration 100.
30in (76.2cm) Käm-
mer & Reinhardt
128 shown wearing
a blue cotton print
dress with white
pinafore and bonnet.

Illustration 98. 30in (76.2cm) Kämmer & Reinhardt 128.
Head incised:

K   ⬡&⬡   R

Simon & Halbig
128
62

Bisque socket head, human hair wig;
blue sleep eyes, feathered eyebrows;
open mouth with two upper teeth,
wobbly tongue; fully-jointed composition body.

Illustration 99. 30in (76.2cm) Kämmer & Reinhardt 128 mark. (The number "62" does not appear in this photo
of the mark.)

Kämmer & Reinhardt 728

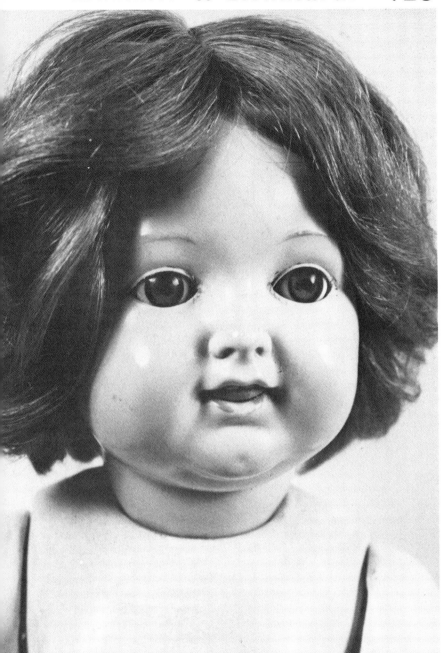

Illustration 101. 17in (43.2cm) Kämmer & Reinhardt 728.

Celluloid socket head, human hair wig; blue sleep eyes, feathered eyebrows; open mouth with two upper teeth, molded tongue; five-piece bent-limb composition body with crier box. *Anita Rae Collection.*

Head incised:

K R

728/7
GERMANY
43/46

Illustration 102. 17in (43.2cm) Kämmer & Reinhardt 728 celluloid head on five-piece bent-limb composition body. *Anita Rae Collection.*

Illustration 103. 17in (43.2cm) Kämmer & Reinhardt 728 celluloid head mark. *Anita Rae Collection.*

Kestner "Century Baby"

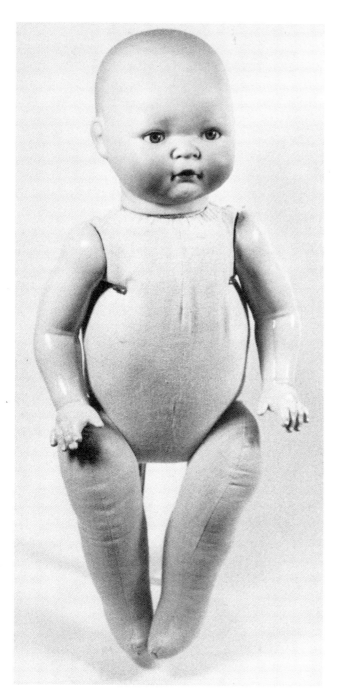

OPPOSITE PAGE:
Illustration 105.
18in (45.7cm) (13in
[33.0cm] head circum-
ference) Kestner, com-
monly called "Century
Baby."
Head incised:
Century Doll Co.
Kestner Germany
Solid dome bisque head
with flange neck, paint-
ed hair; blue sleep eyes,
single stroke eyebrows;
closed, pursed mouth;
cloth body with crier
box; cloth legs, com-
position arms.

Illustration 104. 18in (45.7cm) Kestner "Century Baby"
shown undressed.

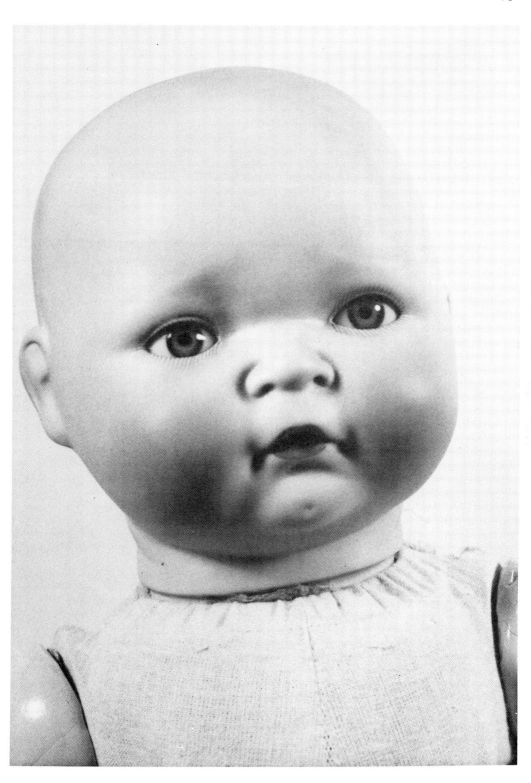

Kestner "Gibson Girl"

Illustration 107. 20in (50.8cm) Kestner "Gibson Girl" shown in a white cotton and lace dress, red silk hat with flowers.

Illustration 106. 20in (50.8cm) Kestner "Gibson Girl" shown undressed.

Illustration 108. 20in (50.8cm) Kestner, commonly called "Gibson Girl."
Shoulder marked: **P made in Germany**
Bisque shoulder head, original plaster pate and blonde mohair wig; blue sleep eyes, single stroke eyebrows; closed mouth; kid body with lower bisque arms.

Kestner 142

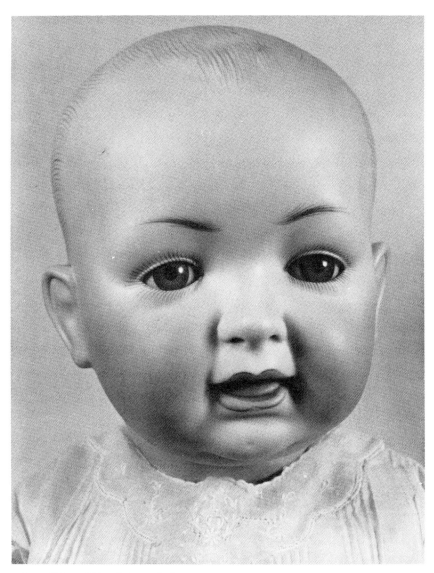

Illustration 109. 22in (55.9cm) (18in [45.7cm] head circumference) Kestner 142.
Head incised: **142**
              15
Solid dome bisque socket head, painted molded hair; blue sleep eyes, feathered eyebrows; open/closed mouth; five-piece bent-limb composition body. *Gladys MacDowell Collection.*

Illustration 110. 22in (55.9cm) Kestner 142 mark. *Gladys MacDowell Collection.*

Illustration 111. 22in (55.9cm) Kestner **142** shown wearing an embroidered pink lawn baby dress. *Gladys MacDowell Collection.*

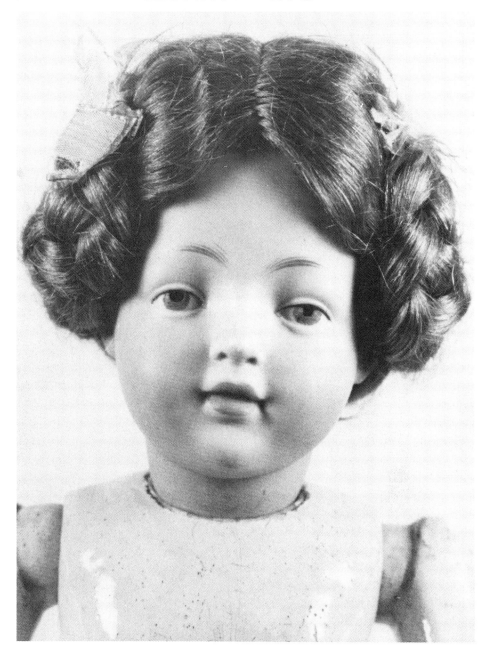

Illustration 112. 11in (27.9cm) Kestner 178.
Head incised: **178**
Bisque socket head, original plaster pate and mohair wig; painted brown eyes, feather-
ed eyebrows; closed mouth; composition body with straight wrists.

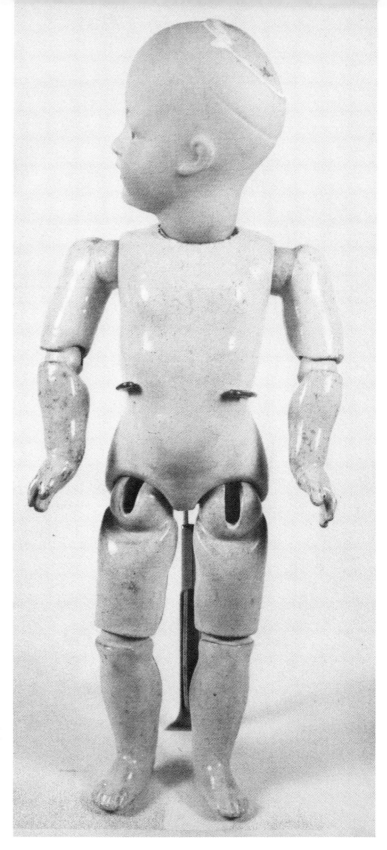

Illustration 113.
11in (27.9cm)
Kestner 178
shown with body
and original
plaster pate.

Illustration 114. 10½in (26.7cm) Kestner 211.

Head incised:

	made in	
B.	Germany.	6
	J.D. K.	
	211.	

Bisque socket head, original plaster pate and mohair wig; brown sleep eyes, feathered eyebrows; open/closed mouth; five-piece bent-limb composition body.

Illustration 115. 10½in (26.7cm) Kestner 211 mark.

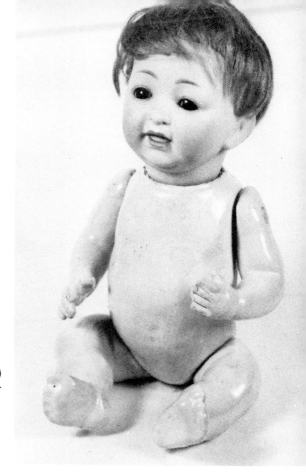

Illustration 116. 10½in (26.7cm) Kestner 211 shown with five-piece bent-limb body.

Illustration 117. 10½in (26.7cm) Kestner 211 wearing a white lawn dress and bonnet.

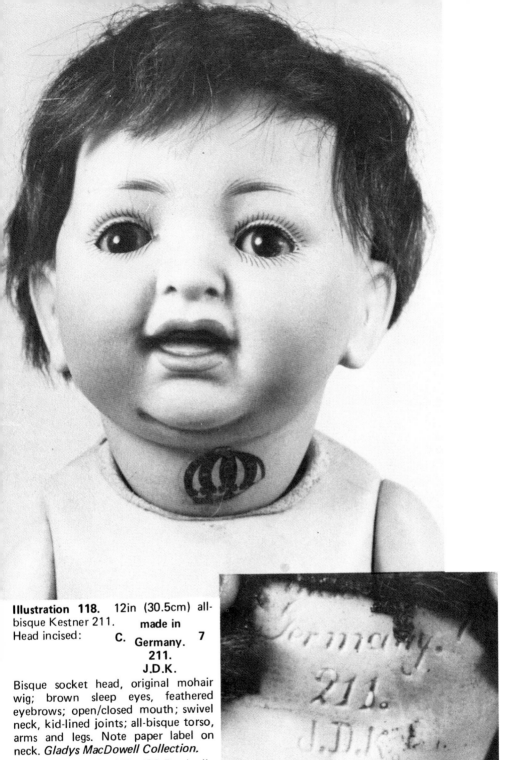

Illustration 118. 12in (30.5cm) all-bisque Kestner 211. **made in** Head incised: **C. Germany. 7 211. J.D.K.** Bisque socket head, original mohair wig; brown sleep eyes, feathered eyebrows; open/closed mouth; swivel neck, kid-lined joints; all-bisque torso, arms and legs. Note paper label on neck. *Gladys MacDowell Collection.*

Illustraiton 119. 12in (30.5cm) all-bisque Kestner 211 mark. (The words "made in" do not appear in this photo of the mark.) *Gladys MacDowell Collection.*

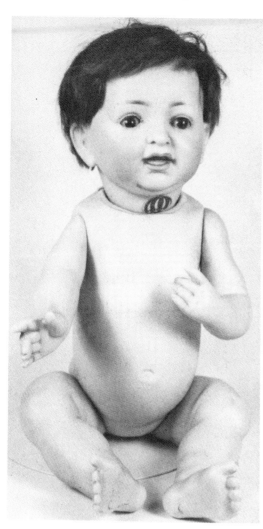

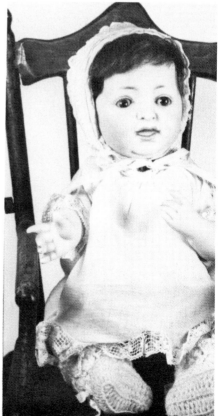

Illustration 120. 12in (30.5cm) all-bisque Kestner 211 shown undressed. *Gladys MacDowell Collection.*

Illustration 121. 12in (30.5cm) all-bisque Kestner 211 shown in lawn dress with lace trim, lawn bonnet and crocheted booties. *Gladys MacDowell Collection.*

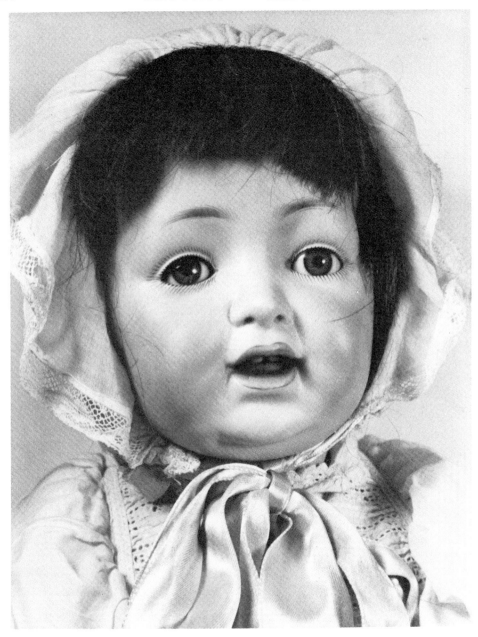

Illustration 122. 22in (55.9cm) Kestner 226.
Head incised:

	made in	
M.	Germany.	16.
	J.D.K.	
	226.	

Bisque socket head, human hair wig; blue sleep eyes, feathered eyebrows; open mouth with two upper teeth, wobbly tongue; five-piece bent-limb composition body. *Private Collection.*

Illustration 123.
22in (55.9cm)
Kestner 226
shown in white
cotton dress with
matching bonnet.
Private Collection

Illustration 124.
22in (55.9cm) Kest-
ner 226 mark. *Pri-
vate Collection*.

Kestner 241

Illustration 125. 22in (55.9cm) Kestner 241.
Head incised:

made in

F½. Germany. 10½.

J.D.K.

241.

Bisque socket head, original blonde human hair wig; blue sleep eyes with lashes, feathered eyebrows; open mouth with upper teeth; jointed composition body. *Gladys MacDowell Collection.*

Illustration 126. 22in (55.9cm) Kestner 241 shown wearing a white cotton blouse and a blue cotton print jumper. *Gladys MacDowell Collection.*

Illustration 127. 22in (55.9cm) Kestner 241 mark. *Gladys MacDowell Collection.*

Kestner *257*

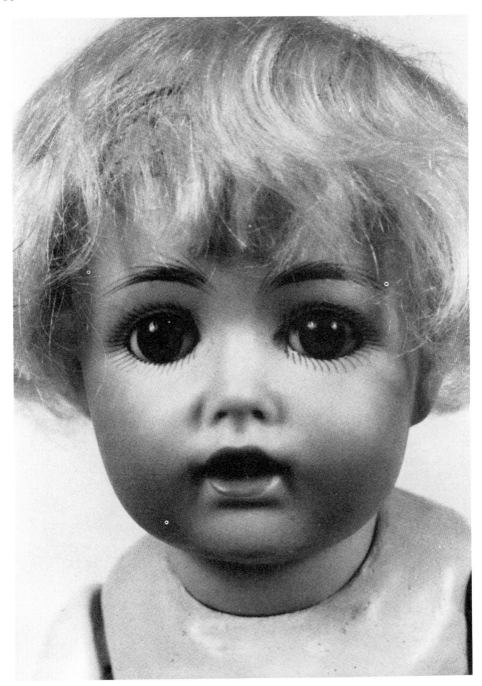

Illustration 128. 7in (17.8cm) Kestner 257.
Head incised: **made in**
                                     Germany.
                                     J.D.K.
                                     257.
Bisque socket head, blonde mohair wig; blue sleep eyes, feathered eyebrows; open mouth, two upper teeth, wobbly tongue. *Lillian J. Mote Collection.*

Illustration 129. 7in (17.8cm) Kestner 257 shown with five-piece bent-limb composition body. *Lillian J. Mote Collection.*

Illustration 130. 7in (17.8cm) Kestner 257 mark. Note red stamped mark on body: "Made in Germany." *Lillian J. Mote Collection.*

Kestner

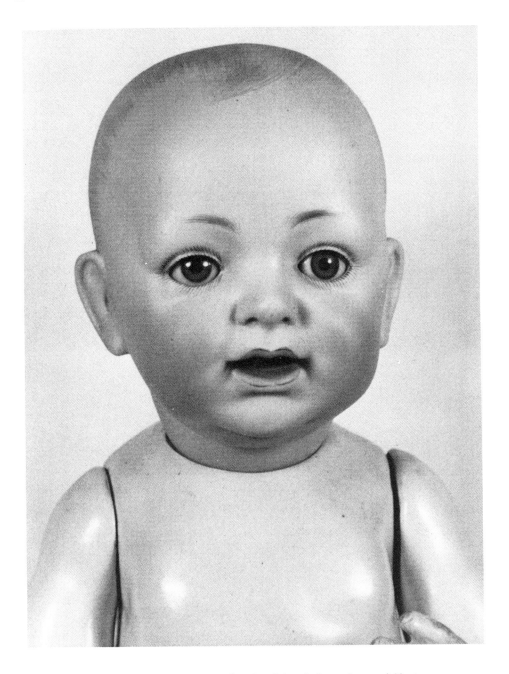

Illustration 131. 16in (40.6cm) (13in [33.0cm] head circumference) Kestner.
Head incised:
J. D. K.
made in 12 Germany
Solid dome bisque socket head, painted molded hair; blue sleep eyes, feathered eyebrows; open mouth, two lower teeth; five-piece bent-limb composition body with voice box.

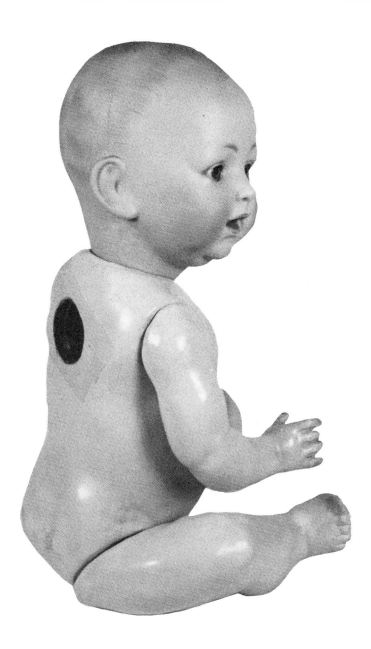

Illustration 132. 16in (40.6cm) Kestner shown undressed. Note opening in back for voice box.

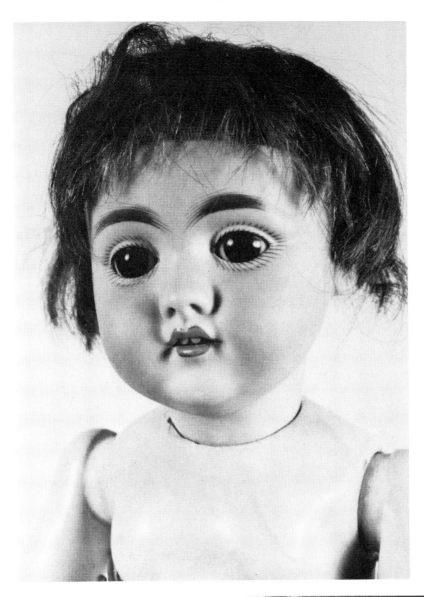

Illustration 133. 15in (38.1cm) Kestner.
Head incised: **made in**
F. Germany   10
Bisque socket head, original plaster pate
with mohair wig; brown sleep eyes,
feathered eyebrows; open mouth with
two upper teeth; composition toddler
body with straight wrists.

Illustration 134.   15in (38.1cm) Kestner
mark.

Illustration 135. 15in (38.1cm) Kestner dressed in pink and white romper suit with felt tam.

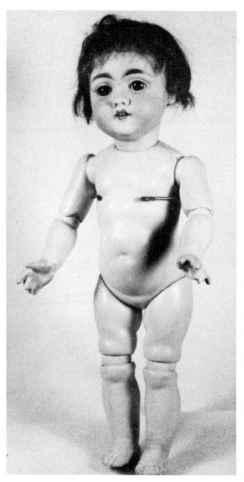

Illustration 136. 15in (38.1cm) Kestner shown with toddler body.

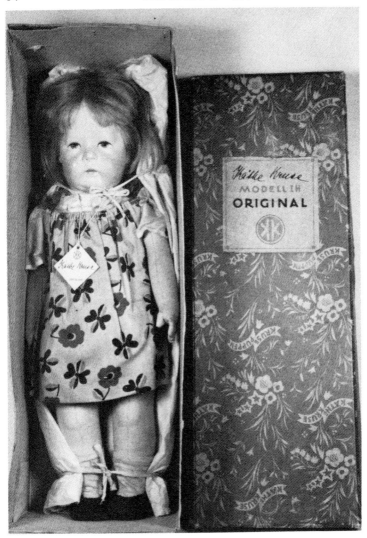

Illustration 137. 17in (43.2cm) Käthe Kruse. All-cloth with painted features, blonde mohair inserted in tiny tufts into cotton cloth scalp; she wears her original printed linen dress, cotton sox and red felt shoes.

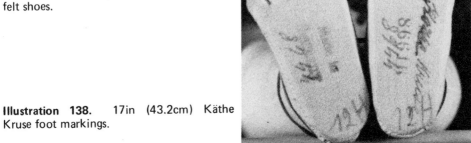

Illustration 138. 17in (43.2cm) Käthe Kruse foot markings.

Illustration 139. Original label of 17in (43.2cm) Käthe Kruse Puppen inside box lid. Translated:

All my dolls are made entirely of cloth. They can be washed with water and soap, although the face should never be scrubbed. They are manufactured in my workshop under my constant personal direction. They are soft, warm and unbreakable and their purpose is:
EDUCATION
TOWARD
MOTHERHOOD
signed Kathe Kruse.

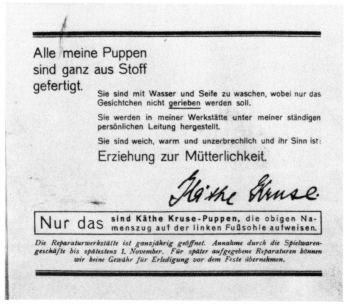

Alle meine Puppen
sind ganz aus Stoff
gefertigt.

Sie sind mit Wasser und Seife zu waschen, wobei nur das Gesichtchen nicht gerieben werden soll.

Sie werden in meiner Werkstätte unter meiner ständigen persönlichen Leitung hergestellt.

Sie sind weich, warm und unzerbrechlich und ihr Sinn ist:

Erziehung zur Mütterlichkeit.

Käthe Kruse.

Nur das sind Käthe Kruse-Puppen, die obigen Namenszug auf der linken Fußsohle aufweisen.

Die Reparaturwerkstätte ist ganzjährig geöffnet. Annahme durch die Spielwarengeschäfte bis spätestens 1. November. Für später aufgegebene Reparaturen können wir keine Gewähr für Erledigung vor dem Feste übernehmen.

Only those are Käthe Kruse-dolls which show the above signature on the left foot sole.

The repair workshop is open year-round. Acceptance through toy shops until November 1 the latest. For repairs submitted later we cannot guarantee completion before the holiday.

Illustration 140. Original Käthe Kruse label on box.

Lori

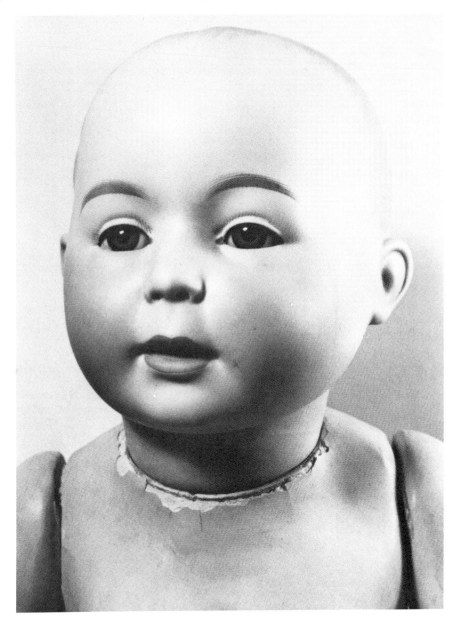

Illustration 141. 23in (58.4cm) *Lori*, made by Swaine & Company.
Head incised and marked:

D
LORI
GESCHUETZT

Solid dome bisque socket head, painted molded hair; blue sleep eyes, feathered
eyebrows; closed mouth; five-piece bent-limb composition body. *Anita Rae Collection.*

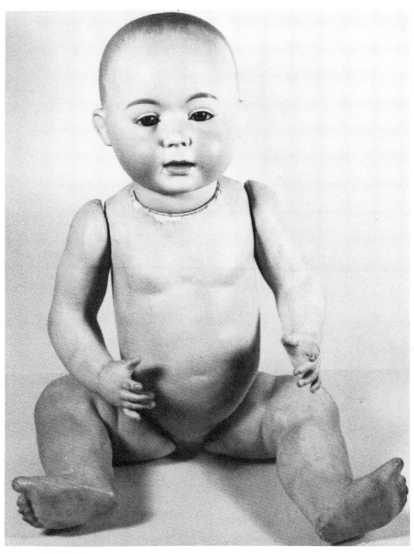

Illustration 142. 23in (58.4cm) *Lori* on five-piece bent-limb composition body. *Anita Rae Collection.*

Illustration 143. 23in (58.4cm) *Lori* mark. *Anita Rae Collection.*

Armand Marseille   Dream Baby

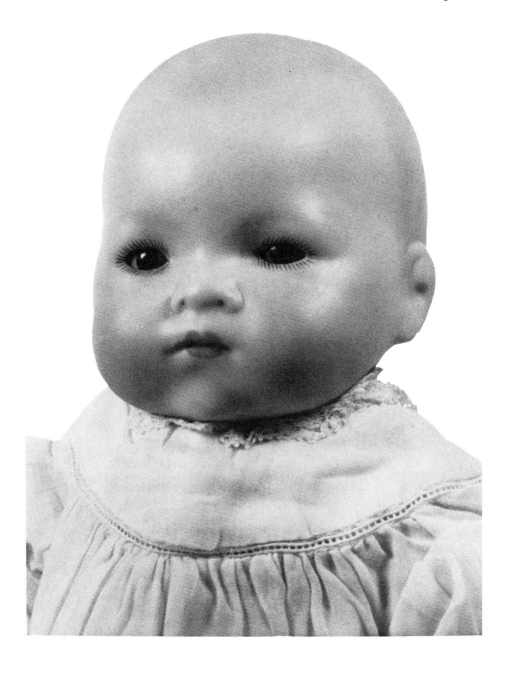

Illustration 144.   13in (33.0cm) (10½in [26.7cm]) head circumference) Armand Marseille *Dream Baby*.
Head incised: **A. M.**
                                        Germany
Solid dome bisque head with flange neck, painted hair; blue sleep eyes, single stroke eyebrows; closed mouth; cloth body with voice box, composition hands.

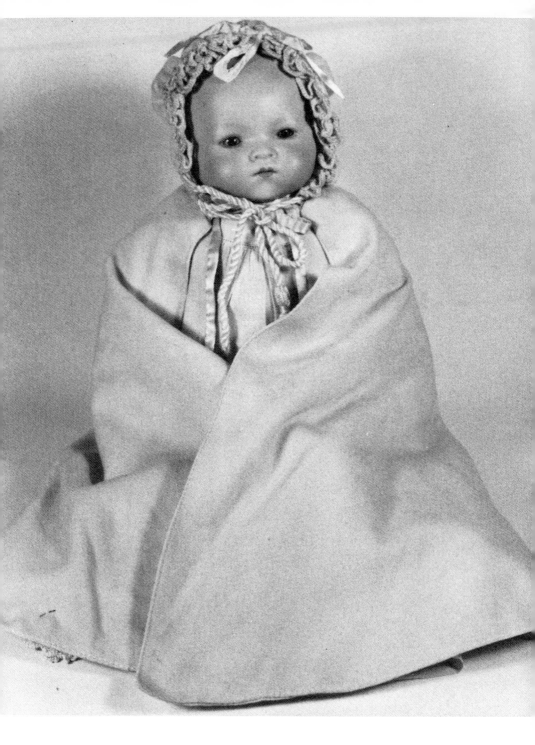

Illustration 145. 13in (33.0cm) Armand Marseille *Dream Baby* dressed in an antique white cotton gown and a beige woolen cape and bonnet.

Armand Marseille 351 Rock-a-bye Baby

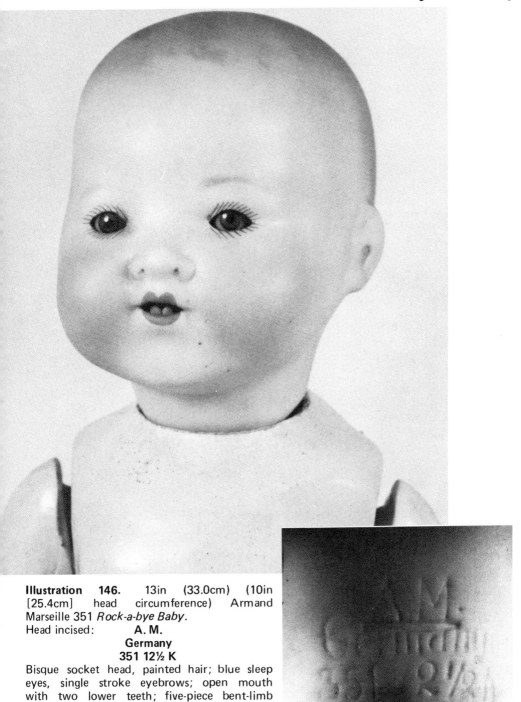

Illustration 146. 13in (33.0cm) (10in [25.4cm] head circumference) Armand Marseille 351 *Rock-a-bye Baby.*
Head incised: A. M.
                   Germany
               351 12½ K
Bisque socket head, painted hair; blue sleep eyes, single stroke eyebrows; open mouth with two lower teeth; five-piece bent-limb composition body.

Illustration 147. 13in (33.0cm) (10in [25.4cm] head circumference) Armand Marseille 351 *Rock-a-bye Baby* mark.

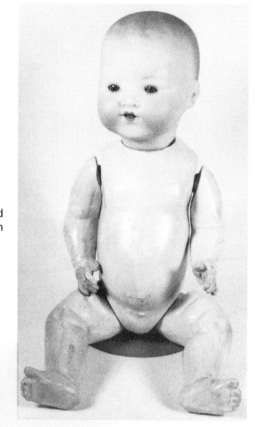

Illustration 148. 13in (33.0cm) Armand Marseille 351 *Rock-a-bye Baby* shown with bent-limb body.

Illustration 149. 13in (33.0cm) Armand Marseille 351 *Rock-a-bye Baby* dressed in white cotton shirt and blue wool pants.

Armand Marseille

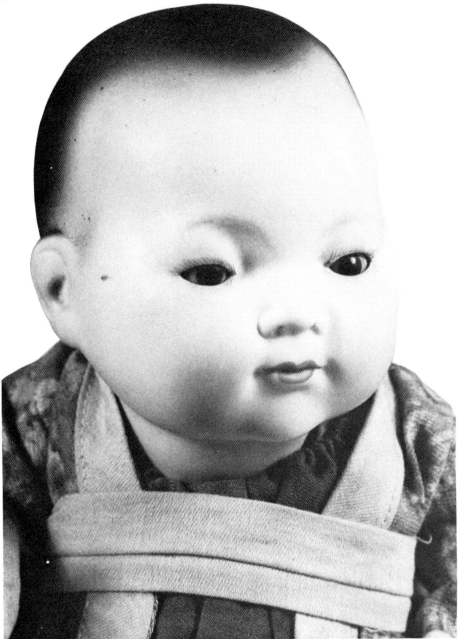

Illustration 150. 11½in (29.2cm) Armand Marseille.
Painted yellow solid dome bisque head, painted black hair; brown sleep eyes, single stroke eyebrows; closed mouth; brown five-piece bent-limb composition body. *Gladys MacDowell Collection.*

Head incised:

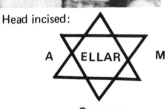

A ELLAR M

Germany
3. K.

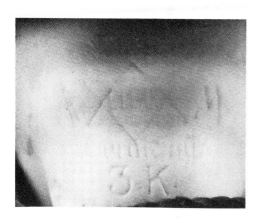

Illustration 151. 11½in (29.2cm) Armand Marseille mark. *Gladys MacDowell Collection.*

Illustration 152. 11½in (29.2cm) Armand Marseille shown undressed. *Gladys MacDowell Collection.*

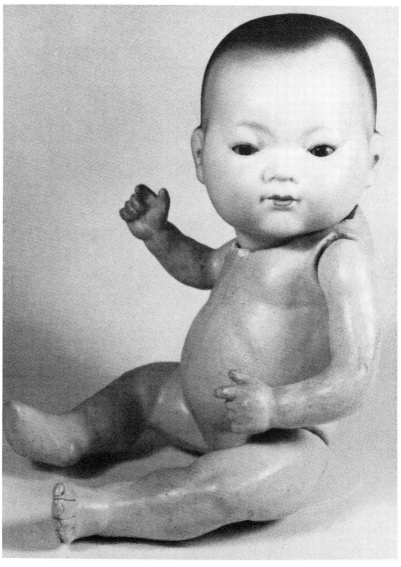

Armand Marseille 1894

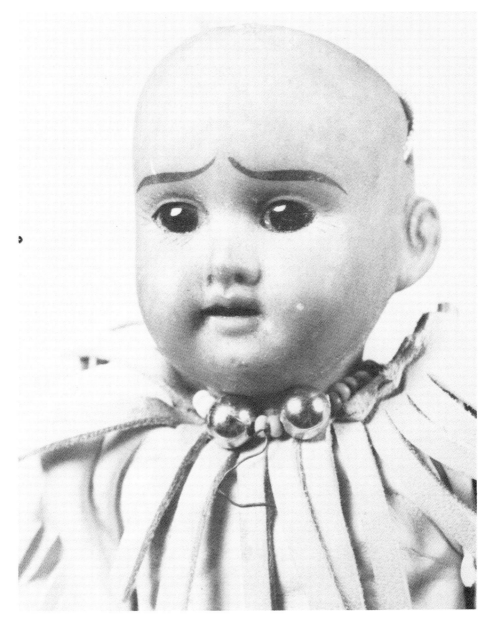

Illustration 153. 8in (20.3cm) Armand Marseille 1894.
Head incised: **1894.**
                                                    A. M. DEP.
                                                    Germany
                                                    11/0.
Painted brown bisque socket head; brown stationary eyes, single stroke eyebrows; open mouth with upper teeth; painted brown five-piece composition body with straight arms and legs; painted yellow shoes. *Gladys MacDowell Collection.*

Illustration 154. 8in (20.3cm) Armand Marseille 1894 wearing his original leather outfit. *Gladys MacDowell Collection*

Illustration 155. 8in (20.3cm) Armand Marseille 1894 mark. *Gladys MacDowell Collection.*

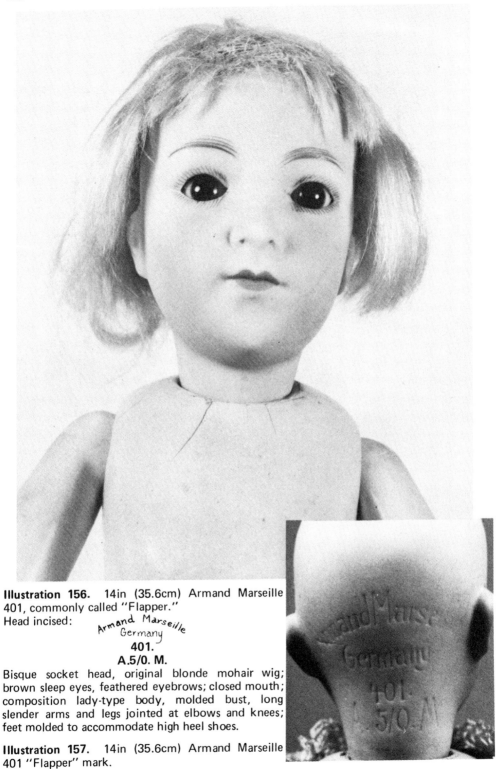

Illustration 156. 14in (35.6cm) Armand Marseille 401, commonly called "Flapper."

Head incised: Armand Marseille
Germany
401.
A.5/0. M.

Bisque socket head, original blonde mohair wig; brown sleep eyes, feathered eyebrows; closed mouth; composition lady-type body, molded bust, long slender arms and legs jointed at elbows and knees; feet molded to accommodate high heel shoes.

Illustration 157. 14in (35.6cm) Armand Marseille 401 "Flapper" mark.

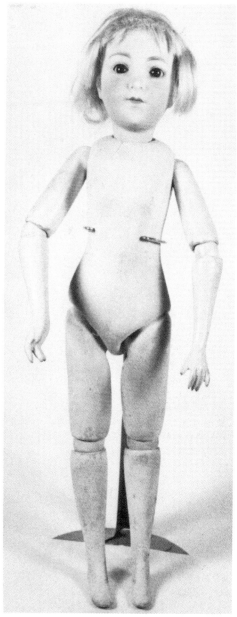

Illustration 158. 14in (35.6cm) Armand Marseille 401 "Flapper" shown in a pink satin with ecru lace outfit and a large straw hat with pink feathers.

Illustration 159. 14in (35.6cm) Armand Marseille 401 "Flapper" shown with lady-type composition body.

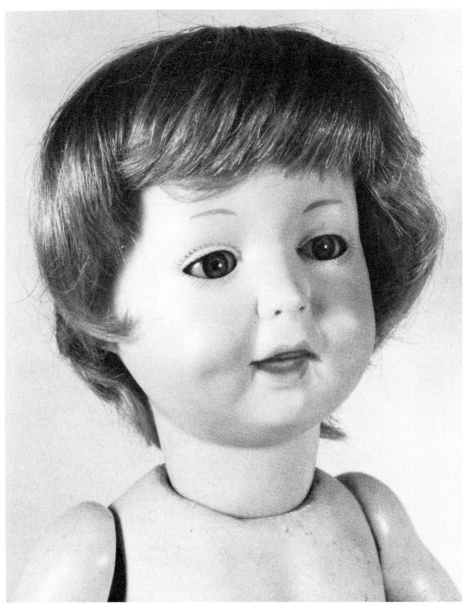

Illustration 160. 14in (35.6cm) Armand Marseille 590.
Head incised: **590.**
                                    A. 3 M.
                                    Germany
                                    D. R. G. M.
Bisque socket head, human hair wig; blue sleep eyes, single stroke eyebrows; open/closed mouth with molded tongue; composition toddler body. Bisque is extremely fine and smooth.

Illustration 161. 14in (35.6cm) Armand Marseille 590 shown in a cotton print dress with a white dotted Swiss pinafore and straw hat.

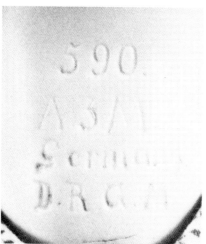

Illustration 162. 14in (35.6cm) Armand Marseille 590 mark.

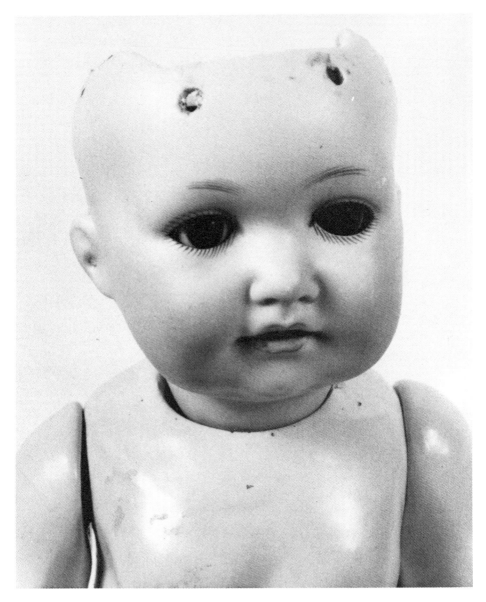

Illustration 163. 13in (33.0cm) (10in [25.4cm] head circumference) Armand Marseille 971a.
Head incised:
971a
A. 1. M.
Germany
Bisque socket head cut to accommodate voice box inside head; brown sleep eyes, feathered eyebrows; open mouth, two upper teeth; five-piece bent-limb composition body.

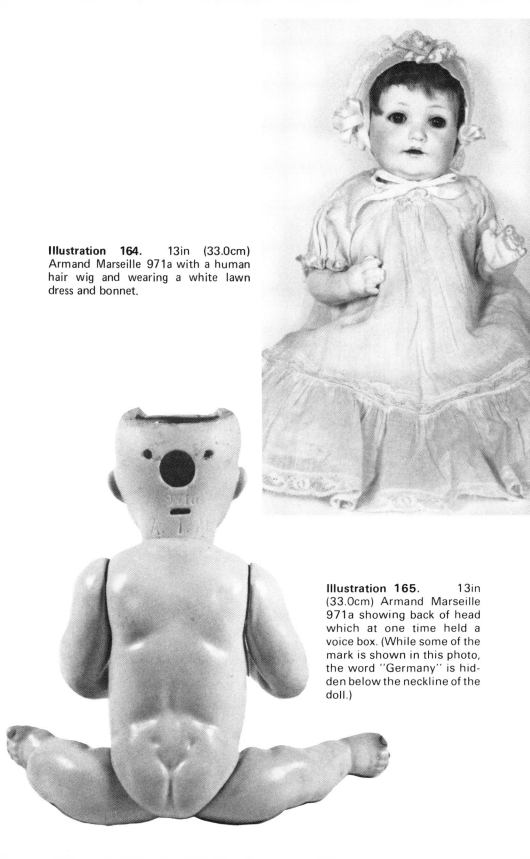

Illustration 164. 13in (33.0cm) Armand Marseille 971a with a human hair wig and wearing a white lawn dress and bonnet.

Illustration 165. 13in (33.0cm) Armand Marseille 971a showing back of head which at one time held a voice box. (While some of the mark is shown in this photo, the word "Germany" is hidden below the neckline of the doll.)

Armand Marseille   975

Illustration 166. 25in (63.5cm) Armand Marseille 975.
Head incised: **Armand Marseille**
                                             A. 975. M.
                                               Germany.
                                                    10.
Bisque socket head, original blonde mohair wig; brown sleep eyes, feathered eyebrows;
open mouth with two upper teeth; fully-jointed composition body.

Illustration 167. 25in (63.5cm) Armand Marseille 975 shown wearing a blue cotton dress and white pinafore and bonnet which accentuate her rosy cheeks.

Illustration 168. 25in (63.5cm) Armand Marseille 975 mark.

Illustration 169. 9½in (24.2cm) Armand Marseille 990.
Head incised: **Armand Marseille**
                 Germany.
                 990.
                 A. 6/0. M.
Bisque socket head, original blonde fur wig; brown sleep eyes, feathered eyebrows; open mouth, two upper teeth; five-piece bent-limb body. He appears to be wearing his original machine-knit blue and pink cotton sweater and pants.

Illustration 170. 9½in (24.2cm) Armand Marseille 990 mark. (The name "Armand Marseille" does not appear in this photo of the mark.)

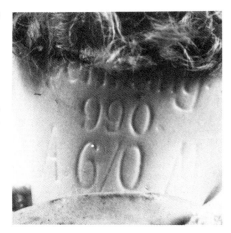

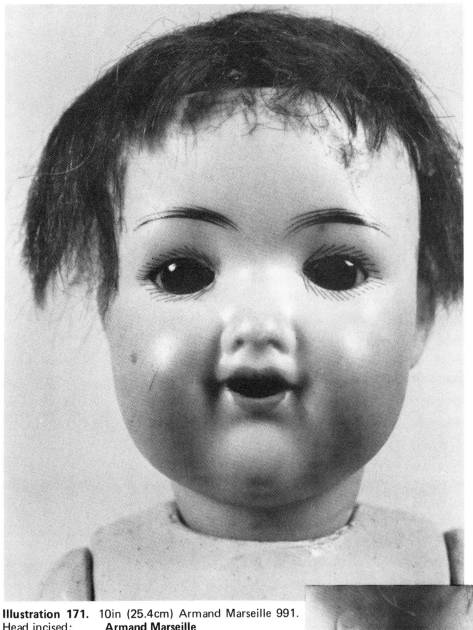

Illustration 171. 10in (25.4cm) Armand Marseille 991. Head incised:

> **Armand Marseille**
> **Germany**
> **991.**
> **A.   6/0.   M.**

Bisque socket head, original dark blonde mohair wig; brown sleep eyes, feathered eyebrows; open mouth with two upper teeth; composition bent-limb body. *Gladys MacDowell Collection.*

Illustration 172. 10in (25.4cm) Armand Marseille 991 mark. (The name "Armand Marseille" does not appear in this photo of the mark.) *Gladys MacDowell Collection.*

Illustration 173. 10in (25.4cm) Armand Marseille 991 shown in a white lawn baby dress with lace and a crocheted bonnet. *Gladys MacDowell Collection.*

Illustration 174. 12½in (31.8cm) Revalo (Maker: Gebrüder Ohlhaver).
Head incised:

Revalo
3.Dep

Bisque socket head, painted molded hair with pink ribbon; blue intaglio eyes, feathered eyebrows; open/closed mouth with molded teeth; wood and composition body with stick legs.

Illustration 175. 12½in (31.8cm) Revalo mark.

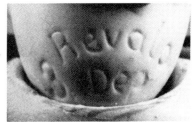

Illustration 176. 12½in (31.8cm) Revalo shown wearing a brown cotton dress, black stockings and black patent leather shoes.

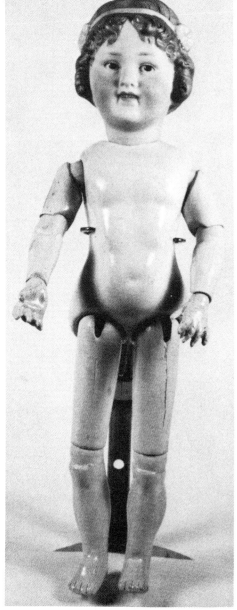

Illustration 177. 12½in (31.8cm) Revalo shown on wood and composition body.

Rheinische Gummi und Celluloid Fabrik Co.

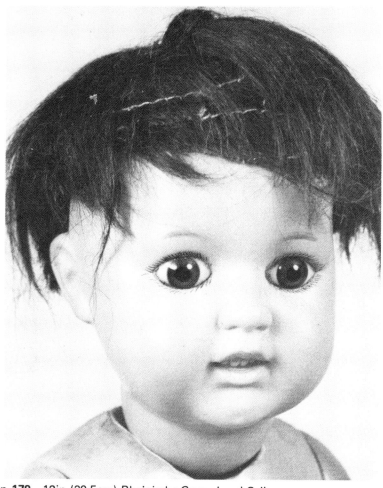

Illustration 178. 12in (30.5cm) Rheinische Gummi und Celluloid Fabrik Co.
Head marked:

GERMANY
30
T

Back marked:

SCHUTZ-MARKE
30
GERMANY

All-celluloid, mohair wig; brown stationary eyes, feathered eyebrows; open/closed mouth with painted teeth; five-piece bent-limb body with two differently shaped arms. *Gladys MacDowell Collection.*

Illustration 179. 12in (30.5cm) Rheinische Gummi und Celluloid Fabrik Co. marks. *Gladys MacDowell Collection.*

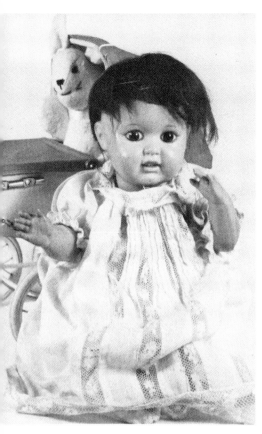

Illustration 180. 12in (30.5cm) Rheinische Gummi und Celluloid Fabrik Co. all-celluloid baby shown in a white lawn and lace dress. *Gladys MacDowell Collection.*

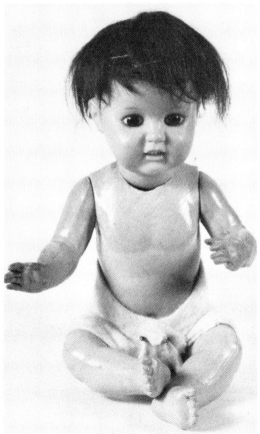

Illustration 181. 12in (30.5cm) Rheinische Gummi und Celluloid Fabrik Co. all-celluloid baby. *Gladys MacDowell Collection.*

Bruno Schmidt "Tommy Tucker"

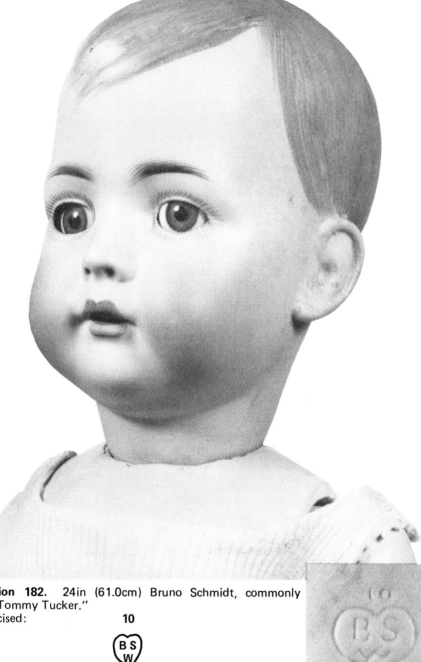

Illustration 182. 24in (61.0cm) Bruno Schmidt, commonly called "Tommy Tucker."
Head incised: **10**

2096
5

Solid dome bisque socket head, painted molded hair; blue sleep eyes, feathered eyebrows; open mouth with two upper teeth; jointed composition body. *Gladys MacDowell Collection.*

Illustration 183. 24in (61.0cm) Bruno Schmidt "Tommy Tucker" mark. *Gladys MacDowell Collection.*

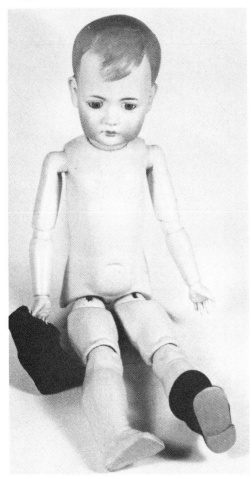

Illustration 184. 24in (61.0cm) Bruno Schmidt "Tommy Tucker" shown with jointed composition body. *Gladys MacDowell Collection.*

Illustration 185. 24in (61.0cm) Bruno Schmidt "Tommy Tucker" dressed in white cotton shirt and dark blue serge suit. *Gladys MacDowell Collection.*

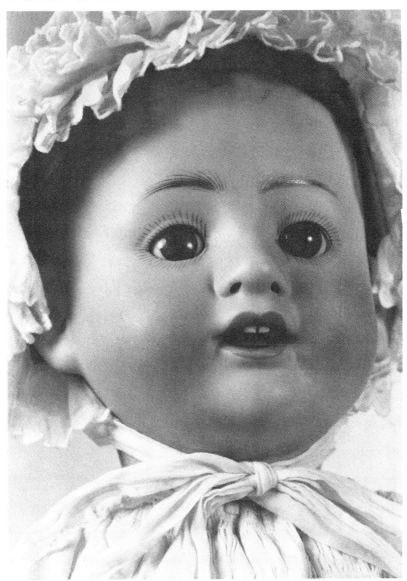

Illustration 186. 17in (43.2cm) Franz Schmidt & Co.
1272. Head incised: **F.S. & Co.**
                              1272/40 Z
                              Deponiert
Bisque socket head, original fur wig; blue sleep eyes,
feathered eyebrows; open mouth with two upper molded teeth, wobbly tongue; pierced nostrils; five-piece
bent-limb composition body with jointed wrists.

Illustration 187. 17in (43.2cm) Franz Schmidt & Co.
1272 mark.

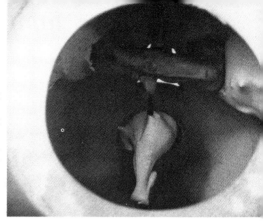

Illustration 188. 17in (43.2cm) Franz Schmidt & Co. 1272 showing inside head mechanism of eyes and tongue. The weight of the eyes is attatched to the wobbly tongue. When doll sleeps, the tongue goes back. When the eyes open, the tongue moves forward.

Illustration 189. 17in (43.2cm) Franz Schmidt & Co. 1272 on five-piece bent-limb composition body. Note the jointed wrists - - an unusual feature on this kind of body. She is wearing a lovely white antique christening gown and bonnet.

Franz Schmidt & Co. 1295

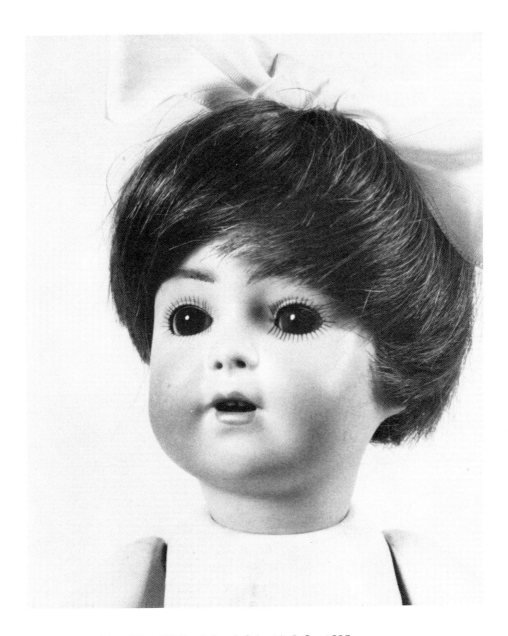

Illustration 190. 10½in (26.7cm) Frank Schmidt & Co. 1295.
Head incised:
                       1295
                       F.S.& C.
                       Made in
                       Germany
                       25
Bisque socket head, human hair wig; brown sleep eyes, feathered eyebrows; open mouth with two upper teeth; pierced nostrils; five-piece composition toddler body with straight arms and legs.

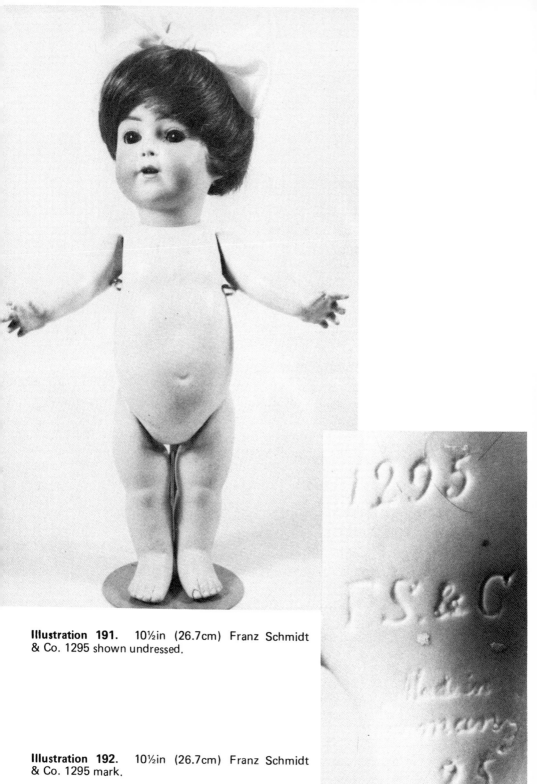

Illustration 191. 10½in (26.7cm) Franz Schmidt & Co. 1295 shown undressed.

Illustration 192. 10½in (26.7cm) Franz Schmidt & Co. 1295 mark.

Illustration 193. 10½in (26.7cm) Franz Schmidt & Co. 1295 identical twins shown wearing cotton print dresses, white pinafores, cotton sox and original leather shoes.

Schönau & Hoffmeister Hanna

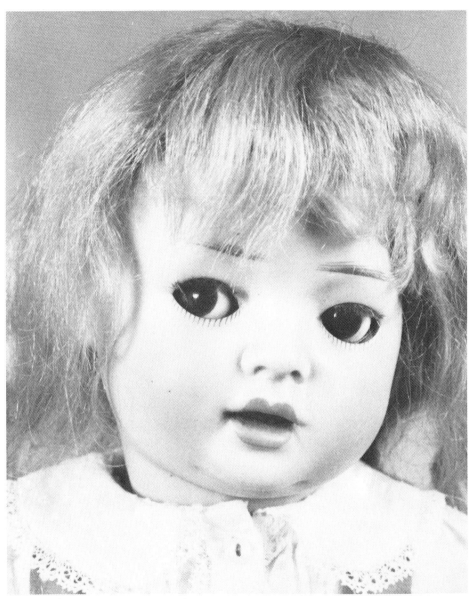

Illustration 194. 16in (40.6cm) Schönau & Hoff-meister *Hanna.*
Head incised:

S ⭐ PB H
Hanna
2

Bisque socket head, blonde mohair wig; brown flirty eyes with lashes, feathered eyebrows; open mouth, two upper teeth; composition toddler body. *Gladys MacDowell Collection.*

Illustration 195. 16in (40.6cm) Schönau & Hoff-meister *Hanna* mark. (The number "2" does not show in this photo of the mark.) *Gladys MacDowell Collection.*

Simon & Halbig 151

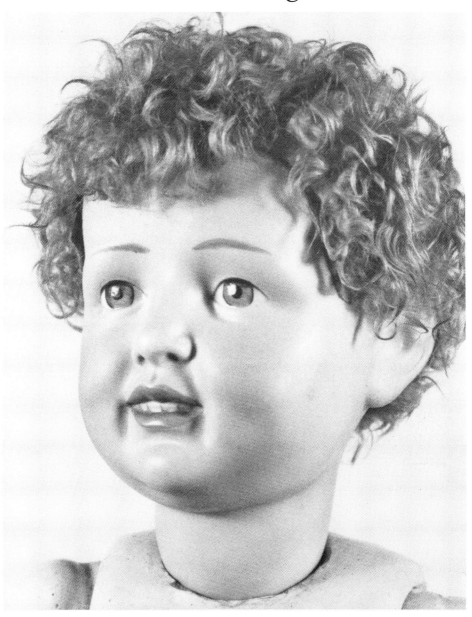

Illustration 196. 21½in (54.6cm) Simon & Halbig 151.
Head incised:

151

S & H

3

Bisque socket head, original red fur wig; painted blue intaglio eyes, single stroke eyebrows; open/closed mouth with painted teeth; jointed composition body. *Gladys MacDowell Collection.*

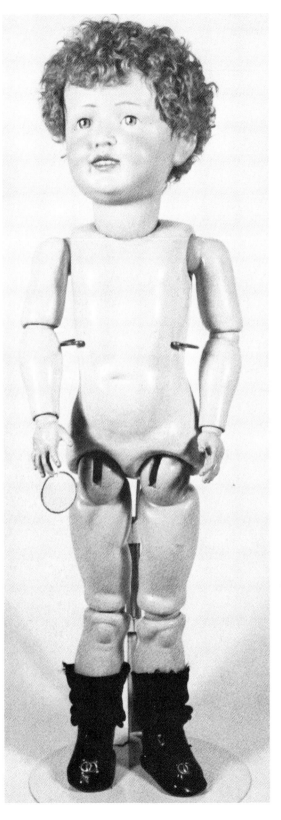

Illustration 197. 21½in (54.6cm) Simon & Halbig 151 shown undressed with jointed composition body. *Gladys MacDowell Collection.*

BELOW: Illustration 198. 21½in (54.6cm) Simon & Halbig 151 mark. *Gladys MacDowell Collection.*

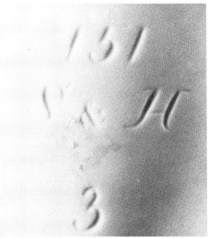

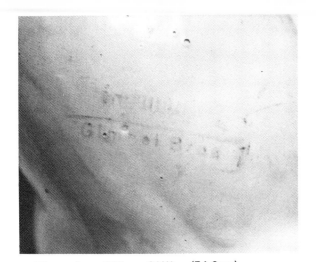

Illustration 199. 21½in (54.6cm)
Simon & Halbig 151 showing mark
on body: **Germany**
Gimbel Bros.
Gladys MacDowell Collection.

Illustration 200. 21½in (54.6cm)
Simon & Halbig 151 dressed in white
cotton shirt and dark blue serge suit.
Gladys MacDowell Collection.

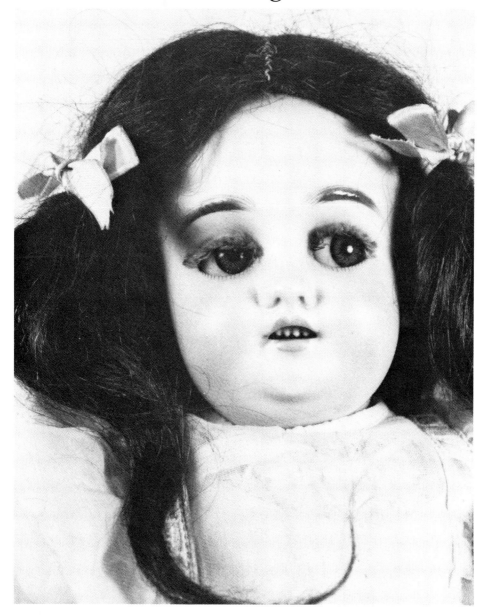

Illustration 201. 13in (33.0cm) Simon & Halbig 1039.
Head incised: **S & H 1039**
                                      DEP
                                        5
                                   Germany
Bisque socket head, original mohair wig; blue flirty eyes with original silk lashes, feathered eyebrows; open mouth, upper molded teeth; pierced ears; jointed composition body with red stamp: **Germany o.**   *Gladys MacDowell Collection.*

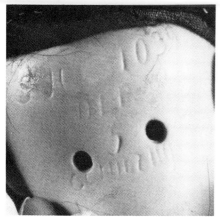

Illustration 202. 13in (33.0cm) Simon & Halbig 1039 mark. *Gladys MacDowell Collection.*

Illustration 203. 13in (33.0cm) Simon & Halbig 1039 shown with her blue organdy dress with pink insertion lace and her underwear. *Gladys MacDowell Collection.*

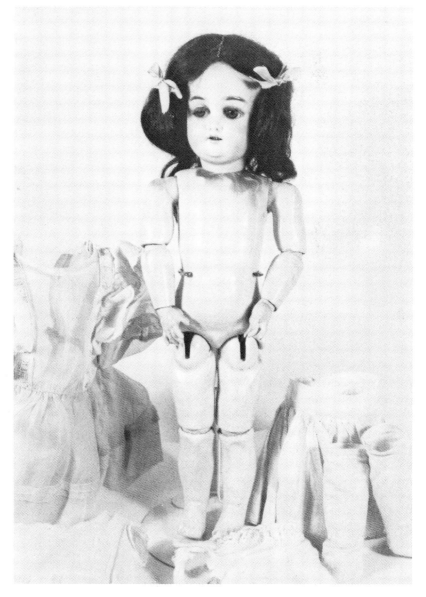

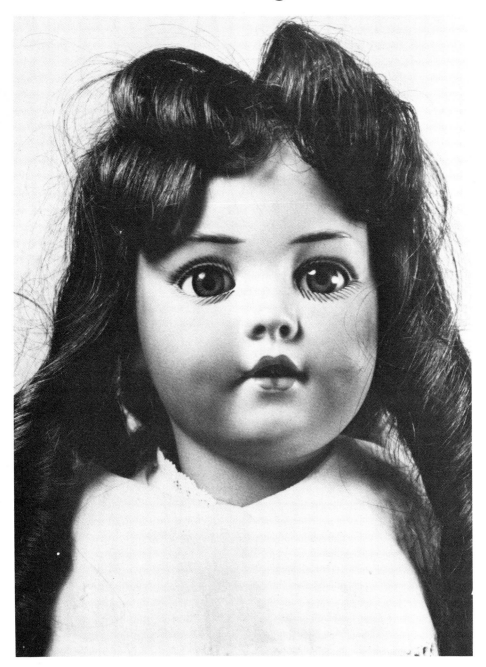

Illustration 204. 19in (48.3cm) Simon & Halbig 1279.
Head incised:

S & H. 1279
DEP.
Germany
8

Bisque socket head, human hair wig; blue sleep eyes, painted molded eyebrows; open mouth with molded upper teeth; pierced ears; jointed composition body. Note deep dimples. *Anita Rae Collection.*

Illustration 205. 19in (48.3cm) Simon & Halbig 1279 mark. *Anita Rae Collection.*

Illustration 206. 19in (48.3cm) Simon & Halbig 1279 shown in an antique white cotton dress and white leather boots. *Anita Rae Collection.*

Illustration 207. 14in (35.6cm) Simon & Halbig 1468, commonly called "Flapper."

Head incised: **1468**

S & H

2

Bisque socket head, original mohair wig; blue sleep eyes with lashes, single stroke eyebrows; closed mouth; pierced ears; lady-type body (flapper) with slender arms and legs which are jointed at elbows and knees; molded bust. *Gladys MacDowell Collection.*

Illustration 208. 14in (35.6cm) Simon & Halbig 1468 "Flapper" mark. *Gladys MacDowell Collection.*

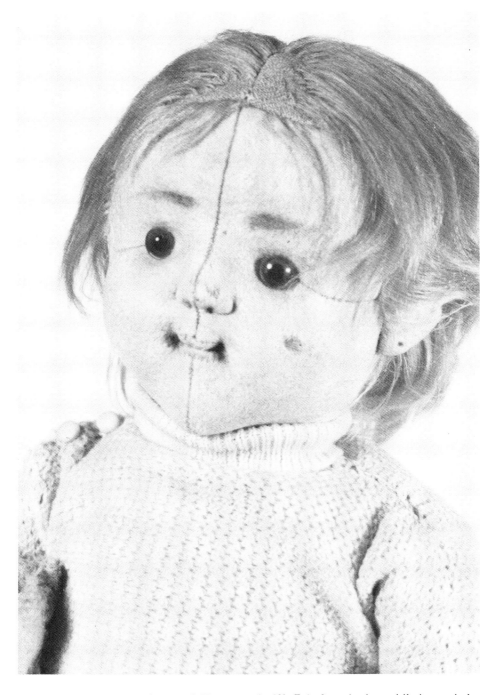

Illustration 209. 18in (45.7cm) Margarete Steiff. Felt face, body and limbs; mohair inserted in tiny tufts into cloth scalp; glass eyes; painted mouth, cheeks, nostrils and eyebrows.

Illustration 210. 18in (45.7cm) Margarete Steiff dressed in woolen machine-knitted undies, wool sweater, felt skirt and combination sox and shoes. Her clothes are believed to be original. She holds a Steiff cat.

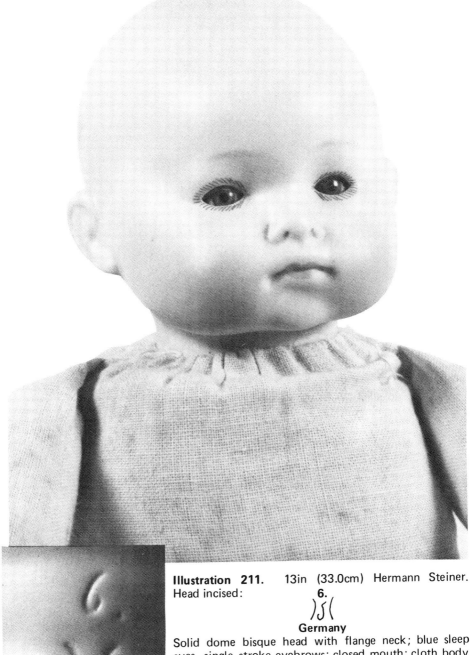

Illustration 211. 13in (33.0cm) Hermann Steiner. Head incised:

6.

)J(

Germany

Solid dome bisque head with flange neck; blue sleep eyes, single stroke eyebrows; closed mouth; cloth body with voice box, celluloid hands.

Illustration 212. 13in (33.0cm) Hermann Steiner mark. (The word "Germany" is barely visible in this photo of the mark.)

Illustration 213. 13in (33.0cm) Hermann Steiner shown on cloth body with celluloid hands.

Illustration 214. 13in (33.0cm) Hermann Steiner dressed in white cotton dress, pink jacket and crocheted bonnet.

Illustration 215. 7in (17.8cm) Strobel & Wilkin Co., commonly called "Googly." Bisque socket head, mohair wig; blue sleep eyes, single stroke eyebrows; closed mouth; five-piece straight-limb composition body with molded and painted sox and shoes.

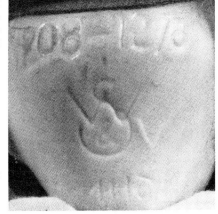

Illustration 216. 7in (17.8cm) Strobel & Wilkin Co. "Googly" mark.

Illustration 217. 7in (17.8cm) Strobel & Wilkin Co. "Googly" shown in a blue cotton dress with lace and a white collar and a crocheted hat.

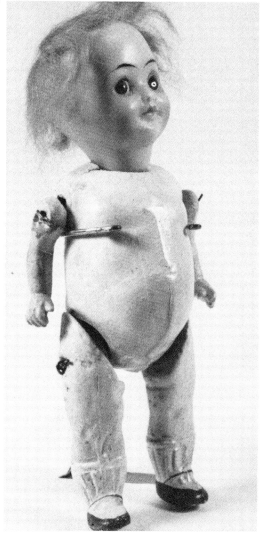

Illustration 218. 7in (17.8cm) Strobel & Wilkin Co. "Googly" shown undressed. Note very crude body.

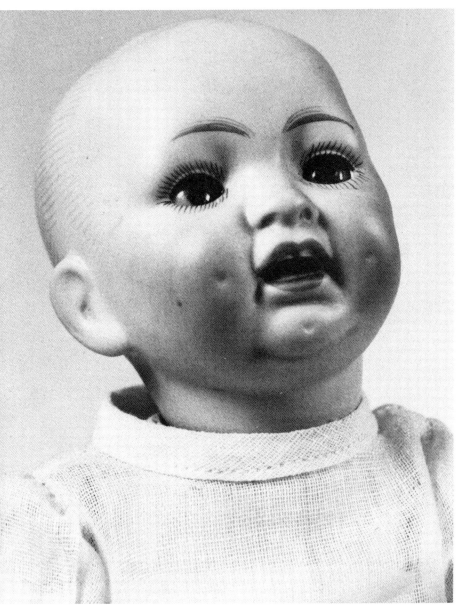

Illustration 219. 9in (22.9cm) Unknown Maker.
Head incised: **3 — 2/o**
Solid dome bisque head, painted hair; blue sleep eyes, feathered eyebrows; open mouth with two upper molded teeth; five-piece bent-limb composition body. *Anita Rae Collection.*

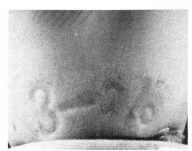

Illustration 220. 9in (22.9cm) Unknown Maker mark. *Anita Rae Collection.*

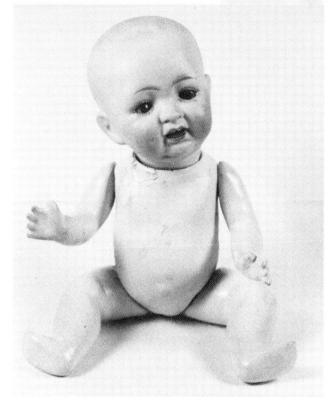

Illustration 221. 9in (22.9cm) Unknown Maker on five-piece bent-limb composition body. *Anita Rae Collection.*

Illustration 222. 9in (22.9cm) Unknown Maker dressed in her original pink voile dress and matching bonnet. *Anita Rae Collection.*

Bibliography

Coleman, Dorothy S., Elizabeth A., & Evelyn J. *The Collector's Encyclopedia of Dolls*. New York: Crown Publishers, Inc., 1973.

Emde-Naegelsbach, Barbara. *Antiquitaeten "Spielzeug"*. Muenchen: Wilhelm Heyne Verlag, 1974.

King, Constance Eileen. *The Collector's History of Dolls*. London: Robert Hale Limited. New York: St. Martin's Press.

Noble, John. *A Treasury of Beautiful Dolls*. New York: Hawthorn Books, Inc. 1971.

Index